Decision-Making for Kids

The Illustrated Guide to Choosing Wisely, Avoiding Mistakes, and Knowing What to Do!

© **Copyright 2025 - All rights reserved.**

The content contained within this book may not be reproduced, duplicated, or transmitted without direct written permission from the author or the publisher.

Under no circumstances will any blame or legal responsibility be held against the publisher, or author, for any damages, reparation, or monetary loss due to the information contained within this book, either directly or indirectly.

Legal Notice:

This book is copyright protected. It is only for personal use. You cannot amend, distribute, sell, use, quote, or paraphrase any part, or the content within this book, without the consent of the author or publisher.

Disclaimer Notice:

Please note the information contained within this document is for educational and entertainment purposes only. All effort has been executed to present accurate, up-to-date, reliable, and complete information. No warranties of any kind are declared or implied. Readers acknowledge that the author is not engaging in the rendering of legal, financial, medical, or professional advice. The content within this book has been derived from various sources. Please consult a licensed professional before attempting any techniques outlined in this book.

By reading this document, the reader agrees that under no circumstances is the author responsible for any losses, direct or indirect, that are incurred as a result of the use of the information contained within this document, including, but not limited to, errors, omissions, or inaccuracies.

Table of Contents

Introduction: Welcome to the world of decision-making! Why learning to make good choices makes you smarter..1

Part I: What Makes a Good Decision? 3

    Chapter 1: The Science of Choice – How We Make Decisions..5

    Chapter 2: Logic vs. Emotion – Thinking vs. Feeling..........7

    Chapter 3: The Decision-Making Blueprint – Steps to a Smart Choice..9

    Chapter 4: The Role of Bias – What Tricks Your Brain?.. 11

    Chapter 5: The Power of Awareness – Noticing When You're About to Make a Bad Choice 13

Part II: Super Smart Thinking Tricks.. 17

    Chapter 6: First Principles Thinking – Breaking Problems into Tiny Pieces 19

    Chapter 7: Occam's Razor – The Easiest Answer is Often the Best..21

    Chapter 8: The Pareto Principle – The 80/20 Rule of Smart Choices..23

    Chapter 9: Second-Order Thinking – Thinking Ahead Before You Act..25

    Chapter 10: Opportunity Cost – Picking One Thing Means Losing Another..28

Chapter 11: The Eisenhower Matrix – What's Urgent vs. What's Important 30

Chapter 12: Regret Minimization – Avoiding "I Wish I Hadn't Done That" Moments 33

Chapter 13: The Fermi Approach – Estimating When You Have No Clue 35

Part III: How to Avoid Thinking Traps 37

Chapter 14: Anchoring Bias – The First Thing You Hear Isn't Always Right 39

Chapter 15: Confirmation Bias – Don't Just Believe What You Want to Be True 41

Chapter 16: Availability Heuristic – Just Because It's Easy to Remember Doesn't Mean It's True 43

Chapter 17: Sunk Cost Fallacy – Why Holding Onto Mistakes Makes Them Worse 46

Chapter 18: Overconfidence Bias – Thinking You Know More Than You Do 49

Chapter 19: The Framing Effect – How Words Can Trick You 52

Chapter 20: Loss Aversion – Why Losing Feels Worse Than Winning Feels Good 55

Chapter 21: Hindsight Bias – Thinking You "Knew It All Along" 58

Chapter 22: Groupthink – When Everyone Just Follows the Crowd 60

Chapter 23: The Dunning-Kruger Effect – Thinking You're a Genius (When You're Not) 62

Part IV: Decision-Making Tools for Kids 65

Chapter 24: The Decision Tree – How to Plan Your Choices Step-by-Step 67

Chapter 25: The Six Thinking Hats – Seeing a Problem in Different Ways 69

Chapter 26: SWOT Analysis – Strengths, Weaknesses, Opportunities, and Threats 72

Chapter 27: Pro/Con Lists Done Right – Why Writing It Down Helps 74

Chapter 28: Scenario Planning – Imagining What Could Go Right (or Wrong) 76

Chapter 29: Pre-Mortem Analysis – Thinking About Failing Before It Happens 79

Chapter 30: Heuristic Shortcuts – Quick Thinking, but Smarter 81

Part V: Emotions and Decision-Making 85

Chapter 31: Self-Regulation – Keeping Your Feelings in Check 87

Chapter 32: Empathy and Decisions – Thinking About Others Before You Choose........................... 89

Chapter 33: The Role of Intuition – When Your Gut Feeling Is (or Isn't) Right................................. 91

Chapter 34: Dealing with Decision Fatigue – Why Too Many Choices Make You Tired................... 94

Chapter 35: Stress-Reduction Techniques – How to Stay Calm Under Pressure..................................97

Chapter 36: The Pause Principle – Stop, Breathe, and Think Before You Act 100

Chapter 37: Handling Regret – Learning from Mistakes Without Feeling Bad Forever 102

Chapter 38: Making Peace with Uncertainty – Accepting That You Can't Know Everything 104

Part VI: Making Decisions with Others 107

Chapter 39: Consensus-Building – Getting a Group to Agree...109

Chapter 40: Avoiding Power Dynamics – When Someone Bossy Takes Over..111

Chapter 41: The Wisdom of Crowds – When More People Make a Smarter Choice 113

Chapter 42: The Delphi Technique – Getting Advice the Right Way 116

Chapter 43: Role Assignment – Giving Everyone a Job in Group Decisions.................................118

Chapter 44: Encouraging Constructive Dissent – Speaking Up When You Disagree 120

Chapter 45: Accountability in Groups – Taking Responsibility for Decisions 122

Part VII: Thinking Ahead for the Future 125

Chapter 46: Game Theory Basics – Making the Best Move in Every Situation 127

Chapter 47: The Long View – Thinking About How Your Choices Affect the Future 129

Chapter 48: Scenario Thinking – Imagining Different Futures Before You Decide 131

Chapter 49: Strategic Patience – Why Waiting Can Lead to Better Decisions 133

Chapter 50: The Power of Experimentation – Testing Your Choices Before Committing 135

Conclusion: What Makes a Great Decision-Maker? How to Keep Practicing Every Day! 137

Appendices 139

1. Quick Reference Guide – A Cheat Sheet for Smart Decision-Making 139

2. Practice Scenarios for Kids – Spot the Decision-Making Mistake Game! 140

3. Tips for Decision-Making – The Top 10 Tricks for Choosing Wisely 143

Here's another book by Quinn Voss that you might like 144

Introduction: Welcome to the world of decision-making! Why learning to make good choices makes you smarter

Hey there! Did you know that every day, you make **hundreds** of decisions? From what to eat for breakfast to what game to play, your brain is *always* making choices.

But here's the big question: **Are you making the BEST choices?**

What Makes a Good Decision?

A good decision is like picking the right path in a maze. Some paths lead to treasure (yay!), while others lead to dead ends (uh-oh!). When you make a smart choice, things work out better. When you make a rushed or bad choice, well... you might end up wishing you had thought it through!

Here's an example:

- Imagine you're at a store, and you see a **cool new toy.** You REALLY want it.
- But wait! If you spend your money now, you **won't** have enough for that awesome game you were saving for.
- What do you do? Buy the toy now or wait for the game?

This is where **smart decision-making** helps! Instead of just acting on what you *want* right now, you think ahead.

Why Does This Matter?

Making great choices can:
- **Save you from mistakes** – No more "I wish I hadn't done that" moments.
- **Help you get what you really want** – Instead of wasting time or money, you make choices that pay off.
- **Make life easier** – When you know how to make smart decisions, you feel more confident and in control.

How This Book Works

This book will teach you the secrets of **smart decision-making!** You'll learn:
- How to avoid common thinking mistakes (your brain can be sneaky!).
- Simple tricks to help you choose wisely.
- Fun ways to test your decision-making skills!

By the time you're done, you'll be a **decision-making pro** — ready to tackle any choice that comes your way!

So, let's jump in and start **choosing wisely!**

Part I: What Makes a Good Decision?

Every day, you make choices—what to eat, what to play, who to talk to. But **how do you know if you're making the best choice?** A good decision isn't just about what feels right *now*—it's about thinking ahead and choosing what's best for **you and your future.** In this section, you'll learn **how your brain makes decisions, what tricks it plays on you, and how to spot bad choices before they happen!**

Chapter 1: The Science of Choice – How We Make Decisions

Every day, you make decisions—what to eat, what to wear, what to play. But have you ever wondered *how* you make those choices?

Let's say you're picking a snack. You see a **chocolate bar** and an **apple**. Which one do you choose?

At first, it seems simple. But inside your brain, two different parts are working:

1. **Fast Thinking** – "Chocolate! It's sweet and delicious! Grab it now!"
2. **Slow Thinking** – "Wait … an apple is healthier and will give me energy. Maybe that's the better choice."

This happens all the time. Sometimes, your brain makes quick choices without thinking too hard. Other times, it slows down and carefully weighs the options.

Why Quick Choices Aren't Always Smart

Long ago, humans needed to make fast decisions to survive. If they saw a wild animal, they didn't stop to think—they *ran!* That fast-thinking instinct is still in your brain today.

But now, most decisions aren't life or death. Instead, they involve **long-term effects** — like saving money, making friends, or choosing to study instead of playing video games.

That's when slow thinking becomes important. **It helps you make smarter choices by thinking ahead.**

The Secret to Better Decisions

Next time you're making a choice, try this:

1. **Pause** – Give yourself a moment to think.
2. **Ask** – "What will happen if I choose this?"
3. **Decide** – Pick the choice that helps you in the long run.

The more you practice, the better your choices will be. And to make even *smarter* decisions, you need to understand the battle between **logic and emotion**—which we'll talk about next!

Chapter 2: Logic vs. Emotion – Thinking vs. Feeling

Imagine you're at a store and see a **new toy** you really want. You have money, but you were saving up for a **bigger toy** later.

Now, two voices start arguing in your head:

- **Your Feelings Say:** "Buy it now! It looks awesome! You'll have fun today!"
- **Your Thinking Brain Says:** "But wait … if you buy this, you won't have enough for the bigger toy later."

This is the battle between **emotion (feelings)** and **logic (thinking)**.

When Emotion Takes Over

Feelings help us enjoy life, but they can also push us into **bad choices**. That's why people sometimes:

- Stay up late watching TV, even though they'll be tired the next day.

- Eat too much candy, even though they'll get a stomachache.
- Buy something impulsively, even though they were saving for something better.

When Logic Takes Over

Logic helps us make smart decisions, but if we **only** use logic, life might feel boring or strict. Imagine if:

- You never ate dessert because it wasn't "necessary."
- You never did anything fun because it wasn't "productive."
- You only made choices based on facts and ignored how you felt.

That wouldn't be fun either! The key is to **balance both**.

How to Balance Logic and Emotion

Next time you have a big decision, try this trick:

1. **Ask two questions:**
    - What do my feelings say?
    - What does my thinking brain say?
2. **Pause and compare both answers.**
3. **Make a choice that makes sense but also feels right.**

The best choices come when **logic and emotion work together.** Now, let's learn some tricks to avoid **thinking mistakes** that can lead to bad decisions!

Chapter 3: The Decision-Making Blueprint – Steps to a Smart Choice

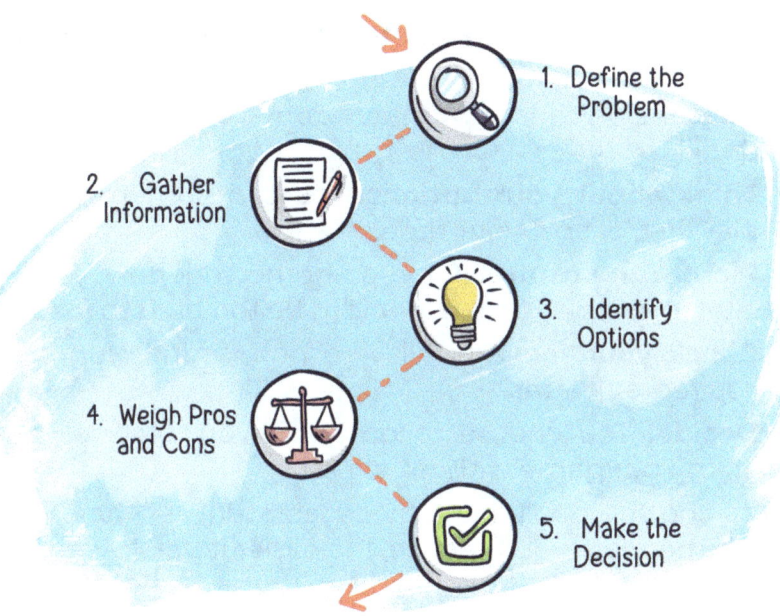

Some decisions are easy — like picking what socks to wear. But others? Not so simple! **Should you join the soccer team or the art club? Should you spend or save your money?** Big choices can feel tricky, but don't worry! There's a simple **blueprint** to help you make **smart decisions every time.**

The 5 Steps to a Smart Choice

1. **Pause.** Instead of deciding *right away*, stop for a moment. Rushed choices often lead to mistakes!
2. **Think about your options.** What choices do you have? List them out. Sometimes, there's more than just "yes" or "no."
3. **Picture the future.** What will happen if you choose each option? Think ahead! Will this choice help you tomorrow, next week, or next year?

4. **Check your feelings.** Are you making this choice just because it feels good **right now**? Or does it also make sense for the future?
5. **Decide and move forward.** Once you've thought it through, **pick the best choice and go with it!**

Let's Practice!

Imagine you're deciding whether to do your homework now or play first.

1. **Pause.** Don't just grab your game controller—stop and think!
2. **Think about your options.** You can do homework first, play first, or split your time.
3. **Picture the future.** If you do homework now, you'll relax later. If you play first, you might be too tired to focus.
4. **Check your feelings.** Playing now sounds fun, but will you regret it later?
5. **Decide.** You choose to do homework first so you can enjoy your game without stress!

Smart choices don't happen by accident — they follow a **plan.** And the more you practice, the easier it gets!

Chapter 4: The Role of Bias – What Tricks Your Brain?

Your brain is amazing—it helps you solve problems, learn new things, and make decisions. But guess what? **Sometimes, your brain plays tricks on you!** These thinking mistakes are called **biases**, and they can lead to **bad decisions** if you don't catch them.

3 Common Biases That Trick You

The First Answer Bias – Your brain likes to **stick with the first thing you hear**, even if it's wrong.

Example: Your friend tells you a new kid is "mean," so you believe it without talking to them yourself.

The "Everyone Else Is Doing It" Bias – Your brain thinks that if others are doing something, it must be a good idea.

Example: Your friends are skipping practice, so you feel like skipping too—even though you know it's a bad choice.

The "It's Always Been This Way" Bias – Your brain assumes that just because something **worked before,** it must be the best choice now.

Example: You always pick the same meal at your favorite restaurant, even though there might be something better!

How to Outsmart These Tricks

- **Stop and Question It** – "Wait... am I choosing this just because it's the first thing I heard?"
- **Think for Yourself** – Just because others do it doesn't mean it's the best choice.
- **Try Something New** – Be open to different ideas instead of doing things the same way every time.

Biases **aren't** bad—they're just shortcuts your brain uses. But if you don't notice them, they can **lead you the wrong way.** And that's why awareness is so important!

Chapter 5: The Power of Awareness – Noticing When You're About to Make a Bad Choice

Have you ever done something and **immediately regretted it**? Maybe you said something mean without thinking, or you picked the wrong answer on a test because you rushed. Afterward, you might have thought, *Why did I do that?*

The answer is simple: **You weren't aware in the moment.**

Awareness is like having a **pause button** for your brain. When you're aware, you can **catch bad decisions before they happen.** But when you're not paying attention, you might make choices you wish you could take back.

How Do People Make Bad Choices?

People usually make bad choices when they act **too fast**, don't think about the future, or let their emotions take over. Here are some common traps:

- **Acting Without Thinking** – You blurt out an answer in class without double-checking, and it turns out to be wrong.
- **Giving In to Pressure** – Your friends want to skip practice, so you join them, even though you know you shouldn't.
- **Letting Feelings Take Over** – You're upset and slam a door, then realize you made things worse.

Bad choices don't just happen. **There are warning signs — if you know where to look.**

Signs You Might Be About to Make a Bad Choice

1. **You feel rushed.** Quick decisions often lead to mistakes. If you feel like you're deciding *too fast*, stop and take a breath.
2. **You feel pressured.** If the only reason you're doing something is because *everyone else is*, that's a sign to pause and think.
3. **You're ignoring that little voice in your head.** If something feels *off*, it probably is. Pay attention to that feeling.
4. **You're only thinking about right now.** Ask yourself, *Will this decision still seem like a good idea tomorrow?* If the answer is no, rethink it.

How to Stay Aware and Make Better Choices

Being aware of your thoughts and actions takes practice, but here are three simple tricks that help:

1. **Use the "Pause and Picture" Rule** – Before making a decision, stop and picture what might happen next. If it looks like trouble, change your choice.
2. **Ask Yourself One Simple Question** – *Will I be happy with this decision later?* If you think you might regret it, take a step back.

3. **Listen to Your Gut Feeling** – If something feels wrong, even if you can't explain why, it's worth taking a second to think before acting.

Let's Practice!

Imagine you're in class, and your friend whispers the answer to a question. You *know* you shouldn't cheat, but you really want to get it right. Before you decide, you:

- **Pause.** Instead of answering right away, you stop and think.
- **Picture the future.** If you cheat, you might get caught. Even if you don't, will you really feel proud of that grade?
- **Check your feelings.** Your gut tells you this isn't the right thing to do.

You decide to answer on your own—even if you get it wrong, at least it's honest. **That's the power of awareness!**

The Secret to Catching Bad Choices Before They Happen

Making smart choices isn't just about *what* you decide—it's about *noticing* when you're about to make a mistake. The next time you feel rushed, pressured, or unsure, **pause and think.** The best decisions happen when you give yourself the chance to make them.

Part II: Super Smart Thinking Tricks

Great decision-makers don't just rely on guesses or feelings—they use smart thinking tricks to **break down problems, see things clearly, and make the best choice.** These simple strategies help you think **faster, smarter, and more creatively** so you can solve problems like a pro. In this section, you'll learn some of the best thinking tools, starting with **First Principles Thinking—one of the smartest ways to solve tough problems!**

Chapter 6: First Principles Thinking – Breaking Problems into Tiny Pieces

Imagine you're trying to build the **fastest toy car ever.** You could just grab the **biggest, shiniest** car at the store … or you could take it apart and **figure out what really makes a car fast.**

First Principles Thinking is about **breaking things down to their smallest parts** and building up from there. Instead of copying what already exists, you ask, *What do I actually need to solve this problem?*

How It Works

Most people solve problems by **doing what's always been done.** But First Principles Thinking helps you find **new and better solutions** by asking three key questions:

1. **What is the problem I need to solve?** (Example: I want to build a faster toy car.)

2. **What are the basic parts of this problem?** (Wheels, weight, aerodynamics, speed.)
3. **How can I improve each part to make the best solution?** (Lighter materials, smoother wheels, better design.)

Why This Works

Instead of just copying what's already out there, **you rebuild the solution from the ground up.** People who think this way invent **new ideas, smarter solutions, and better ways to do things!**

Real-Life Example: The Wright Brothers

The Wright Brothers, who invented the first airplane, didn't just copy birds or hot-air balloons. They **broke flying down into tiny parts**—lift, control, and speed—and tested each part until they created a working airplane!

Try It Yourself!

Let's say you want to get better at **saving money.** Instead of just saying, *"I need to stop spending so much,"* use First Principles Thinking:

- **Break it down.** Where is my money going? Snacks? Toys? Games?
- **Find new solutions.** Can I pack a snack instead of buying one? Can I trade games instead of buying new ones?
- **Test and improve.** Try your ideas, see what works, and adjust!

The Secret to Smarter Problem-Solving

First Principles Thinking **helps you invent new ideas, solve problems better, and make smarter choices.** Instead of guessing or copying what others do, break things down, rebuild them, and find the **best** way forward.

Chapter 7: Occam's Razor – The Easiest Answer is Often the Best

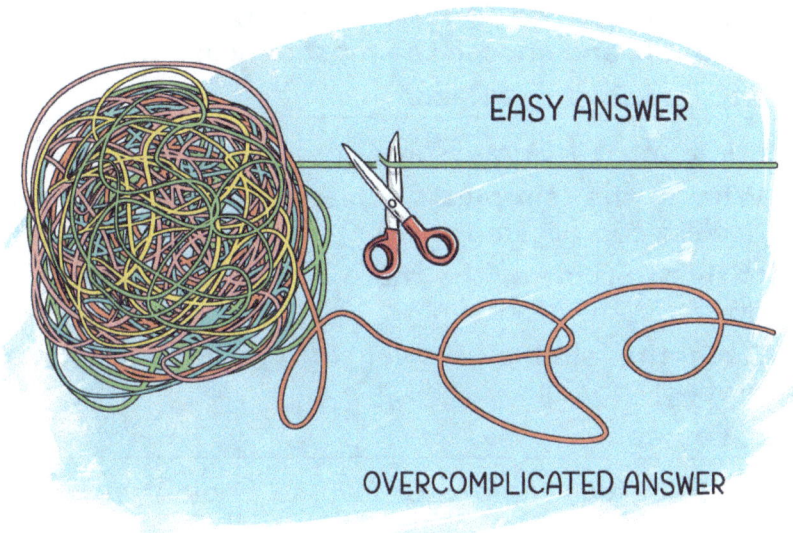

Imagine you wake up and see your bike is missing from the yard. What happened?

You come up with two ideas:

1. **A sneaky group of expert bike thieves used high-tech tools to steal it in the middle of the night.**
2. **You forgot to put it in the garage, and someone simply took it.**

Which one seems more likely?

Occam's Razor is a thinking trick that says: **The simplest explanation is usually the right one.** Instead of overcomplicating things, it helps you focus on the answer that makes the most sense.

Why Do People Ignore the Simple Answer?

People love exciting stories. If something goes wrong, the brain wants to come up with **big, dramatic reasons**—even when the real answer is simple.

For example:
- You text your friend, and they don't reply. Your brain **could** think: *They're mad at me! Maybe I did something wrong!*
- Or ... they just left their phone at home.

Instead of jumping to wild conclusions, **Occam's Razor helps you stop, think, and choose the most logical answer.**

How to Use Occam's Razor

Next time you're trying to solve a problem, ask yourself:

1. **What's the simplest explanation?** (Not everything needs a complicated answer.)
2. **Is there proof for the more complicated idea?** (If not, don't assume it's true.)
3. **Does the simple answer fit the facts?** (If yes, it's probably right!)

Try It Yourself!

Let's say you can't find your favorite book. Which is more likely?

- **Theory 1:** A secret book thief snuck in and took it.
- **Theory 2:** You left it in your backpack.

Occam's Razor reminds you to check your backpack first—because **most of the time, the easiest answer is the right one.**

The Secret to Thinking Clearly

When something happens, don't jump to wild conclusions. **Look for the simplest explanation first.** It will save you time, worry, and a lot of unnecessary confusion!

Chapter 8: The Pareto Principle – The 80/20 Rule of Smart Choices

Imagine you have **10 toys,** but you only play with **2 of them** all the time. Or you have **a huge pile of clothes,** but you mostly wear the **same few favorites.**

That's the **Pareto Principle,** also called the **80/20 Rule**—it means that in many situations, **a small amount of effort or things create most of the results.**

How the 80/20 Rule Works

The Pareto Principle says that **about 80% of what happens comes from just 20% of the effort.**

Here are some examples:
- **In school:** You might learn **80% of a subject** from **20% of the lessons** that explain it best.
- **In sports:** 20% of your practice drills** make you **80% better.**
- **In video games: 20% of your best strategies** help you win **80% of the time.**

The key to **working smarter, not harder** is figuring out which 20% makes the biggest difference.

How to Use the Pareto Principle

Instead of trying to **do everything**, focus on the **small actions that give you the biggest results.**

1. **Find What Works Best.** – Which study method helps you the most? Which practice drill improves your game the fastest?
2. **Do More of That.** – Spend more time on what's actually helping, and less on things that don't.
3. **Cut Out Wasted Effort.** – If something isn't helping much, stop focusing on it.

Try It Yourself!

Let's say you have **a big test** coming up. You could:
- **Read the entire textbook (takes forever).**
- **Focus on the 20% of notes that explain 80% of what you need to know.**

Which one is smarter? **The second choice saves time and still helps you succeed.**

The Secret to Working Smarter

The Pareto Principle helps you **find what matters most and focus on it.** Instead of working harder on everything, **find the small things that make the biggest impact — and do more of those!**

Chapter 9: Second-Order Thinking – Thinking Ahead Before You Act

Imagine you're given a choice: **Would you rather eat a giant bowl of ice cream or a plate of vegetables?**

Your first thought might be, **"Ice cream! It's sweet and delicious!"** But what happens next? If you eat too much, you might get a stomach-ache. If you eat veggies, you'll feel strong and energized later.

This is where **Second-Order Thinking** comes in. Instead of only thinking about **what happens now**, it helps you think about **what happens next—and after that.**

First-Order vs. Second-Order Thinking

Most people stop at **first-order thinking**, which is only about what happens *right away*. But **second-order thinking** asks, *"And then what?"*

Let's look at an example:
- **First-Order Thinking:** "I'll stay up late to play video games because it's fun."
- **Second-Order Thinking:** "And then what? I'll be tired tomorrow. I won't focus in class. Maybe I should sleep instead."

The second-order thinker **sees the future effects of their choices.**

Why It's Important

People who only think about **right now** often make **bad decisions** because they don't see the bigger picture. Second-Order Thinking helps you:

- Avoid **regret** (so you don't think, *Why did I do that?*)
- Plan **smarter** (so you make choices that help you later).
- Outthink problems before they happen.

How to Use Second-Order Thinking

Next time you make a choice, ask yourself:

1. **What happens next?** (*If I do this, what's the immediate result?*)
2. **And then what?** (*What will happen later because of this?*)
3. **Is that what I really want?** (*Will this choice help me in the long run?*)

Try It Yourself!

You're about to **spend all your money on candy.** Stop and think:

- **First-Order Thinking:** "I get candy, and it tastes great!"
- **Second-Order Thinking:** "And then what? My money is gone. I won't be able to buy the cool thing I was saving for."

Now you can make a **smarter choice!**

The Secret to Smarter Decisions

Second-Order Thinking helps you **see the future effects of your choices.** Instead of only thinking about *right now*, ask yourself, *"And then what?"* This one simple question can help you make **better decisions every day.**

Chapter 10: Opportunity Cost – Picking One Thing Means Losing Another

Imagine you have **one movie ticket** and two choices:
1. Watch a fun action movie with your best friend.
2. Watch a cool science movie that teaches you something new.

You can only pick **one**. No matter what you choose, **you're also giving something up.** That's called **Opportunity Cost**—whenever you pick one thing, you're losing the chance to do something else.

What Is Opportunity Cost?

Opportunity Cost is **the hidden cost of every decision**. It's not about money—it's about what you *could have* done instead.

- If you **spend your allowance on a toy**, the cost is **not being able to buy something later**.

- If you **watch TV all afternoon**, the cost is **losing time to do homework or play outside**.
- If you **eat all your snacks today**, the cost is **not having any for tomorrow**.

Why It Matters

Many people don't think about **what they're losing** when they make a choice. But smart decision-makers **always consider the trade-offs.**

- Before spending money, ask: *Is this the best way to use it?*
- Before using time, ask: *Will I regret not doing something else?*
- Before saying yes to something, ask: *What am I saying no to?*

How to Use Opportunity Cost in Everyday Life

Next time you have a choice, stop and ask:
1. **What am I choosing?** (*What do I get?*)
2. **What am I giving up?** (*What's the cost?*)
3. **Which one is more valuable to me?** (*Is this the best use of my time, money, or energy?*)

Try It Yourself!

You're deciding whether to **play video games for an hour** or **practice a new skill** (like drawing or soccer).

- **Choice 1:** Play video games.
- **Choice 2:** Practice and get better at something.

If you choose video games, the **opportunity cost** is missing the chance to improve your skills. If you choose practice, the **opportunity cost** is not playing your game.

The Secret to Better Choices

Every decision has a cost—even if you don't see it right away. Smart decision-makers **think ahead** and choose what gives them the **best** result in the long run. Next time you make a choice, remember: **picking one thing means losing another — so, choose wisely!**

Chapter 11: The Eisenhower Matrix – What's Urgent vs. What's Important

Imagine you have **homework to finish**, **a birthday party to plan**, and **a new game you really want to play.** Everything feels like it needs to be done **right now**—but does it?

Some things feel urgent, but **not everything is equally important.** That's where the **Eisenhower Matrix** comes in—it helps you decide **what to do first, what can wait, and what isn't worth your time.**

Urgent vs. Important: What's the Difference?

- **Urgent** tasks need attention **right now**—like answering a ringing phone.
- **Important** tasks help you in the **long run**—like studying for a test or practicing a skill.

Some things are **both urgent and important** (like finishing a project before the deadline). But others **only feel urgent** (like checking every new text message).

How the Eisenhower Matrix Works

This tool helps you **sort your tasks** into four categories:
1. **Important & Urgent – Do It Now!**
    - Homework due today
    - Studying for a test tomorrow
    - Helping someone in an emergency
2. **Important but Not Urgent – Plan It!**
    - Practicing a sport or hobby
    - Saving money for something big
    - Building a good friendship
3. **Urgent but Not Important – Limit It!**
    - Replying to random messages
    - Watching a new video because everyone else is
    - Doing small tasks that don't really matter
4. **Not Urgent & Not Important – Skip It!**
    - Scrolling through your phone with no goal
    - Playing a game just because you're bored
    - Worrying about things you can't change

How to Use It in Real Life

Next time you feel **overwhelmed with things to do**, try this:
1. **Make a list of everything on your mind.**
2. **Sort each task** into one of the four categories.
3. **Start with the important and urgent tasks first.**
4. **Plan time for the important but not urgent tasks.**
5. **Cut down or remove the things that aren't worth your time.**

Try It Yourself!

You have a big test coming up, but your friend just texted asking if you want to play a game.

- **Important & Urgent:** Studying for your test.
- **Important but Not Urgent:** Practicing a hobby for fun.
- **Urgent but Not Important:** Replying to your friend's text right away.
- **Not Urgent & Not Important:** Scrolling through memes instead of studying.

The Eisenhower Matrix helps you **focus on what really matters** so you don't waste time on things that don't.

The Secret to Getting More Done

Not everything that feels urgent is important. **Smart decision-makers focus on what truly matters.** When you manage your time wisely, you'll get more done *and* have time for fun—without stress!

Chapter 12: Regret Minimization – Avoiding "I Wish I Hadn't Done That" Moments

Have you ever made a decision and **immediately wished you could take it back**? Maybe you stayed up late watching YouTube videos and felt exhausted the next day. Or maybe you quit a game too early, only to find out your team made an amazing comeback.

Regret happens when we **make choices without thinking ahead**. But what if you could make decisions that **you won't regret later**? That's where **Regret Minimization** comes in! It helps you **think about the future before making a choice** so you don't end up saying, *"I wish I had done things differently."*

How to Use Regret Minimization

Before making a decision, ask yourself:
1. **How will I feel about this tomorrow?**
2. **How will I feel about this in a week?**
3. **How will I feel about this in a year?**

If you think your future self **will be happy** with your choice, go for it! If you think your future self **might regret it**, it's time to rethink.

Let's Try It!

Imagine you have a big school project due tomorrow, but your friend just invited you to go to the arcade.

- **Tomorrow:** You'll feel stressed trying to finish the project at the last minute.
- **A week from now:** You might regret your bad grade.
- **A year from now:** You probably won't even remember skipping the arcade, but you *will* remember struggling with your schoolwork.

Thinking ahead, you might **decide to finish the project first** and plan another day to go to the arcade. **That's how Regret Minimization helps you make smarter choices!**

Why This Works

Most regrets come from **acting too quickly** without considering what happens next. Regret Minimization **helps you slow down and think about the future** before making a decision.

The Secret to Fewer Regrets

Next time you're about to make a choice, **imagine your future self looking back.** If you think you'll **be proud of your decision**, go for it! If not, take a step back and make a different choice. **Your future self will thank you!**

Chapter 13: The Fermi Approach – Estimating When You Have No Clue

What if someone asked you, **"How many jellybeans fit in a giant jar?"** or **"How many people are playing soccer right now in your country?"**

You probably don't know the exact answer—but that doesn't mean you can't make a **smart guess!**

The **Fermi Approach** is a way of solving big or confusing problems by **breaking them into smaller, easier steps.** It helps you make good estimates —even when you have no clue where to start!

How the Fermi Approach Works

Instead of guessing randomly, the Fermi Approach asks:
1. **What do I already know?** (Even if it's not the exact answer, start with something related.)

2. **Can I break this into smaller parts?** (Big problems are easier to solve in steps.)
3. **Can I make a reasonable estimate?** (Think logically instead of randomly guessing.)

Let's Try It!

Imagine you want to estimate **how many slices of pizza are eaten in your city every day.**

- **Step 1: Start with what you know.** You know that many people like pizza and that most pizzas have about **8 slices.**
- **Step 2: Break it down.** How many people live in your city? Let's guess **500,000.** Maybe half of them eat pizza each day—so **250,000 people.**
- **Step 3: Make a smart estimate.** If each person eats **3 slices** on average, that's **250,000 × 3 = 750,000 slices of pizza every day!**

You might not get the exact number, but you're a lot **closer to the real answer** than a wild guess!

Why This Works

The Fermi Approach helps you:

- **Think logically instead of guessing randomly.**
- **Break big problems into smaller, solvable parts.**
- **Make good estimates even when you don't have all the facts.**

The Secret to Smarter Thinking

Next time you face a big question and don't know the answer, **don't panic!** Instead, use the Fermi Approach: **Start with what you know, break it down, and estimate step by step.** You'll be surprised how close you can get!

Part III: How to Avoid Thinking Traps

Your brain is amazing, but sometimes it **takes shortcuts that lead to mistakes.** These mistakes, called **thinking traps**, can trick you into making bad decisions without even realizing it! In this section, you'll learn about the **sneaky ways your brain can fool you** — and how to **outsmart these tricks** so you can make **better, smarter choices.** Let's start with one of the biggest thinking traps: **Anchoring Bias!**

Chapter 14: Anchoring Bias – The First Thing You Hear Isn't Always Right

Imagine you walk into a store and see a **cool backpack** with a price tag of **$100**. That sounds **expensive!** But then, you see another backpack that costs **$50**. Suddenly, the second one seems like a **great deal!**

But wait—**is it really a good deal, or does it just seem that way because of the first price you saw?**

This is called **Anchoring Bias.** It happens when your brain **gets stuck on the first piece of information you see**, even if it's not the most important.

How Anchoring Bias Tricks You

Your brain loves to **compare things** instead of judging them on their own. The first number, fact, or idea you see **sticks in your mind like an anchor**, making everything else seem better or worse in comparison.

Here's another example:
- A store lists a **video game at $60**, but then says, **"Now only $40!"** You feel like you're saving $20, but maybe the game was **never worth $60 to begin with!**
- A friend tells you a movie is **"the best ever,"** so you expect it to be amazing. But is it really, or did their opinion **anchor** your thinking?

Why It Matters

Anchoring Bias can lead to **bad decisions** because you're comparing things to **the first number or idea you saw, not what actually makes sense.** It can make you **spend more money, trust wrong information, or make choices too quickly.**

How to Avoid the Trap

1. **Slow down.** Just because something seems like a good deal doesn't mean it is. **Take a step back and think!**
2. **Compare wisely.** Instead of comparing something to the first number you see, **ask if it's truly worth it.**
3. **Look for more information.** Before deciding, **check other prices, opinions, or facts** so you don't get stuck on the first one.

Try It Yourself!

Let's say your friend tells you their favorite pizza place is **"the best in town."** Do you:
- **A:** Believe them without trying other places?
- **B:** Try different pizza places and decide for yourself?

The smart choice? **Option B!** That way, you're not just **anchored** to what they said—you're thinking for yourself!

The Secret to Avoiding Decision-making Traps

Anchoring Bias **tricks you into comparing instead of thinking.** Next time you see a "deal," hear an opinion, or get a big first number, **pause and ask: Is this really the best choice, or is my brain just stuck on the first thing I saw?**

Chapter 15: Confirmation Bias – Don't Just Believe What You Want to Be True

LOOK AT ALL THE FACTS

Have you ever been **sure** you were right about something—only to find out later you were wrong? Maybe you thought a test would be easy, so you only studied a little... and then realized too late that you **should have studied more.**

This happens because of **Confirmation Bias**—a sneaky thinking trap where your brain **only looks for information that proves what you already believe** and ignores everything else.

How Confirmation Bias Tricks You

Your brain **likes being right.** So instead of searching for the full truth, it tries to **find "proof" that your first thought was correct—even if it isn't!**

Here's an example:
- You think **your lucky socks** help you win soccer games. Every time you win while wearing them, you think, *See? They work!*
- But when you lose a game, you **ignore it** or make excuses: *That didn't count because it was raining.*
- Instead of seeing the whole picture (*winning depends on skill, practice, and teamwork*), your brain **only notices the times that "prove" you were right.**

Why This Is a Problem

Confirmation Bias can lead to **bad decisions** because it **blocks you from seeing the full truth.** It makes you:
- Ignore facts that don't match what you already believe.
- Make decisions based on feelings instead of reality.
- Miss chances to learn and grow.

How to Avoid This Trap

1. **Ask yourself, "Could I be wrong?"** Instead of looking for proof that you're right, look for **facts on both sides.**
2. **Check different sources.** If you hear something online, don't just believe the first thing you see—**look at different opinions and facts.**
3. **Listen to people who disagree with you.** Instead of arguing, **try to understand their point of view.** You might learn something new!

Try It Yourself!

Imagine you think **cats are better than dogs.** Instead of only watching videos about why cats are great, try looking up **why dogs are great too.** If you still like cats more, that's fine—but at least you **gave both sides a fair chance!**

The Secret to Smarter Thinking

Confirmation Bias **makes your brain look for "proof" that you're right—even when you're not.** To make better choices, **look at all the facts, not just the ones you like!** The more open you are to learning, the smarter your decisions will be.

Chapter 16: Availability Heuristic – Just Because It's Easy to Remember Doesn't Mean It's True

Imagine you're watching the news, and you see a story about a shark attack at the beach. Later, when your friends invite you to go swimming in the ocean, you say, **"No way! I don't want to get eaten by a shark!"**

But here's the thing—**shark attacks are extremely rare.** You're actually more likely to get hurt **by a falling coconut** than by a shark! So why does your brain make you think shark attacks are common?

This is called the **Availability Heuristic**—a thinking trap where your brain **believes something is more likely just because it's easier to remember.**

How the Availability Heuristic Tricks You

Your brain likes to **take shortcuts.** Instead of looking up facts, it **relies on the first thing that pops into your mind.**

Here are some ways this can trick you:

- **You see a plane crash on the news and think flying is dangerous.** But actually, planes are much safer than cars!
- **You remember one time you failed a test and think you're bad at math.** But you've done well on plenty of tests—you just don't remember them as easily!
- **You hear about one person getting sick from a certain food and decide never to eat it.** But millions of people eat it safely every day.

Why This Is a Problem

The Availability Heuristic makes you **trust your memory more than actual facts.** This can lead to:

- **Unnecessary fear** (*like thinking every stranger is dangerous just because of a scary news story*).
- **Bad decisions** (*like avoiding a great opportunity because of one bad experience*).
- **Wrong beliefs** (*like thinking something is true just because you heard it a lot*).

How to Avoid This Trap

1. **Ask, "Is this really common, or does it just feel that way?"** Just because you hear about something often **doesn't mean it happens a lot.**
2. **Look at the numbers.** If you're scared of something, **check the real facts** instead of going with what you remember.
3. **Think about the good, not just the bad.** Your brain remembers negative things more easily, so **make sure you're looking at the full picture.**

Try It Yourself!

Let's say your friend thinks roller coasters are unsafe because they heard about **one accident.** Instead of agreeing right away, you check the facts and find out that **millions of people ride roller coasters safely every year.** Now you can **decide based on facts, not just fear.**

The Secret to Avoiding This Trap

The Availability Heuristic **makes you believe things are more common just because they're easier to remember.** Next time your brain jumps to a conclusion, **pause and check the facts.** The real answer might surprise you!

Chapter 17: Sunk Cost Fallacy – Why Holding Onto Mistakes Makes Them Worse

Imagine you're playing a board game, but **halfway through, you realize you don't like it.** You'd rather do something else, but you think, *I've already spent an hour playing... I might as well finish.*

Or maybe you start reading a book, but it's **boring.** Instead of putting it down, you tell yourself, *I've already read half of it—I can't stop now!*

This is called the **Sunk Cost Fallacy.** It's a thinking trap where **you keep doing something just because you've already spent time, money, or effort on it—even if it's not the best choice anymore.**

How the Sunk Cost Fallacy Tricks You

Your brain doesn't like to **waste things.** If you've **put in time or effort**, you feel like quitting means **you've lost everything.**

Here's how this thinking trap works:

- **You spend money on a movie ticket, but the movie is terrible.** Instead of leaving, you think, *I paid for this, so I have to stay.*
- **You keep playing a video game you don't enjoy anymore** because you've already played for hours.
- **You eat food you don't like** just because you already paid for it.

Why This Is a Problem

The Sunk Cost Fallacy **makes you stick with bad decisions** just because you've already spent something on them. But here's the truth:

- Time you've already spent is gone—you can't get it back.
- Money you've already used is spent—you can't unspend it.
- Forcing yourself to finish something you don't enjoy just wastes more time!

How to Avoid This Trap

1. **Ask, "Would I start this now?"** If you weren't already doing it, **would you choose to do it?** If not, it's okay to stop.
2. **Focus on the future, not the past.** Instead of thinking, *What have I already spent?* ask, *What's the best choice moving forward?*
3. **Let go of bad choices.** Just because you **started something** doesn't mean you have to **finish** if it's not worth it anymore.

Try It Yourself!

Let's say you've been **watching a TV show, but you don't like it anymore.**

- **Stuck in the trap:** *I've already watched three seasons, so I have to finish!*
- **Smart choice:** *That time is already spent—I can stop and do something better with my time.*

How to Avoid Getting Stuck

The Sunk Cost Fallacy **makes you afraid to quit, even when quitting is the smarter choice.** Next time you feel stuck, **forget what you've already spent and focus on what's best for your future.** Sometimes, the smartest decision is to **walk away!**

Chapter 18: Overconfidence Bias – Thinking You Know More Than You Do

Have you ever been **super sure** about something — only to find out later that you were **completely wrong**? Maybe you thought you knew all the answers to a test but got a lower grade than expected. Or maybe you were sure you could beat your friend in a video game without practicing, only to lose big time.

This happens because of **Overconfidence Bias** — a thinking trap where **you believe you know more than you actually do.**

How Overconfidence Bias Tricks You

Your brain **likes to feel smart** and **in control.** But sometimes, it **tricks you into thinking you know everything**—even when you don't!

Here are some common examples:

- **You don't study for a test** because you assume you already know everything—then you struggle with the harder questions.
- **You jump into a new game without reading the rules** and quickly realize you don't know how to play.
- **You guess an answer instead of double-checking it**—and get it wrong.

Being confident is **good**, but **being overconfident** can lead to mistakes.

Why This Is a Problem

Overconfidence Bias makes you:

- **Take shortcuts** instead of preparing properly.
- **Ignore advice** from people who might actually know more.
- **Underestimate challenges**, making things harder for yourself.

How to Avoid This Trap

1. **Ask, "Do I really know this, or am I just guessing?"** If you're not 100% sure, take a moment to check.
2. **Listen to feedback.** If someone corrects you, don't ignore them—see if they might be right.
3. **Be open to learning.** Even if you think you know a lot, there's always more to discover.

Try It Yourself!

Imagine you're about to race your friend in a new game. You think, *I don't need to learn the rules—I'll figure it out!*

- **Stuck in the trap:** You lose because you didn't take the time to learn the game first.
- **Smart choice:** You ask about the rules and **practice first**—giving you a much better chance to win.

How To Stay Curious

Overconfidence Bias **makes you think you know more than you actually do.** The best way to avoid it? **Stay curious, double-check your facts, and always be open to learning!** Smart people don't just assume they're right—they take the time to **make sure.**

Chapter 19: The Framing Effect – How Words Can Trick You

Imagine you're at the grocery store, and you see two signs on cartons of juice:

- **Option 1:** "90% real fruit juice!"
- **Option 2:** "Only 10% sugar water!"

Which one would you pick?

Most people choose **Option 1** because "90% real fruit juice" *sounds* better. But guess what?

Both are the exact same thing! The way something is **described** can **change how your brain sees it—even when the facts don't change.**

This is called the **Framing Effect**, and it's a sneaky trick that **makes you feel differently about something just because of how it's worded.**

How the Framing Effect Tricks You

Your brain reacts differently depending on **how something is said**, not just what it means. Let's look at another example:

- **A doctor says, "This medicine helps 80 out of 100 people feel better."** You feel hopeful.
- **A doctor says, "This medicine doesn't work for 20 out of 100 people."** You feel unsure.

Both statements mean the **same thing**, but one *sounds* much better than the other. That's the **Framing Effect** at work!

Why This Is a Problem

The Framing Effect can make you:

- **Believe something is better or worse than it really is.**
- **Trust a deal or discount that sounds amazing—even if it's not that special.**
- **Get scared by how something is worded, even if the facts aren't so bad.**

How to Avoid This Trap

1. **Flip the wording.** If something sounds too good (or too bad) to be true, **try saying it the opposite way** and see if it still makes sense.
2. **Look at the actual facts.** Instead of reacting to how something is **described**, check what's actually true.
3. Ask, **"Is this trying to change how I feel?"** If something is **framed to sound exciting or scary**, stop and think before believing it.

Try It Yourself!

Imagine you're buying a snack, and the label says:

- **Option 1:** "80% fat-free!"
- **Option 2:** "Contains 20% fat."

Which one sounds healthier? The first one *sounds* better, but **both are exactly the same!** That's the Framing Effect in action.

How to See Through the Trick

The Framing Effect **changes how things sound without changing the truth.** Next time you hear something that seems *too good or too scary,* **pause and look at the facts.** When you see through the trick, you make **smarter, clearer choices!**

Chapter 20: Loss Aversion – Why Losing Feels Worse Than Winning Feels Good

Have you ever found a dollar on the ground? That feels pretty awesome! But now imagine you had a dollar in your pocket, and you **lost** it. That would feel **way worse** than finding a dollar felt good.

That's because of **Loss Aversion**—a sneaky brain trick that makes **losing something feel much worse than gaining the same thing.**

How Loss Aversion Tricks You

Your brain **hates losing** so much that it sometimes **makes bad choices just to avoid it.**

Here are some examples:

- **You keep playing a board game you don't like** just because you already spent an hour on it. (*I don't want to waste my time!*)

- **You hold onto toys you don't play with** because giving them away *feels like losing something—even if you never use them!*
- **You wait in a long line for a ride** even though another ride has no wait—because you don't want to "lose" the time you've already spent waiting.

Why This Can Be a Problem

Loss Aversion **makes you focus too much on what you might lose instead of what you could gain.** It can cause you to:

- **Stay stuck doing things you don't enjoy.**
- **Make choices based on fear instead of what's actually best.**
- **Say "yes" to things just because you don't want to miss out.**

How to Stop This Thinking Trap

1. **Ask, "Would I make this choice if I were starting fresh?"** If the only reason you're sticking with something is because you don't want to "lose," that's a sign to rethink your choice.
2. **Think about what you'll gain instead.** If you stop playing a boring game, now you have time for a fun one! If you give away an old toy, someone else can enjoy it, and you have more space for things you actually use.
3. **Remember: Losing isn't always bad.** Sometimes letting go of one thing makes space for **something even better.**

Try It Yourself!

Imagine you're **reading a book that's boring.**

- **Loss Aversion says:** *I already read 50 pages, so I have to finish it.*
- **Smart thinking says:** *That time is already gone—why not spend the rest of my time reading something fun instead?*

How to Make Better Choices

Loss Aversion makes losing **feel worse than it really is.** But sometimes, **letting go of one thing helps you get something even better!** Next time you don't want to give something up, **ask yourself if it's really worth keeping — or if it's time to move on.**

Chapter 21: Hindsight Bias – Thinking You "Knew It All Along"

Have you ever watched a game and, after your team lost, thought, **"I knew they were going to lose!"** Or maybe you guessed an answer on a test and got it wrong, then told yourself, **"I knew I should have picked the other one!"**

That's called **Hindsight Bias**—a sneaky brain trick that makes you **think you knew something was going to happen... even though you actually didn't.**

How Hindsight Bias Tricks You

Your brain loves to feel **smart and in control.** So when something happens, it **rewrites the past** to make it seem like you "knew it all along"—even if you didn't!

Here's how this thinking trap works:

- **Before a race:** You aren't sure who will win.
- **After the race:** You say, *"I knew that runner would win!"* (Even though you really didn't!)

Or:
- **Before a test:** You aren't sure of an answer.
- **After the test:** You think, *"I knew I should have picked the other answer!"* (But if you really *knew*, you would have picked it the first time!)

Why This Can Be a Problem

Hindsight Bias **makes you feel like you were right all along**, which can **stop you from learning from mistakes.** If you always think, *"I knew that was going to happen,"* you might:
- Ignore what you actually learned.
- Forget that some things are just unpredictable.
- Miss a chance to improve your decision-making.

How to Avoid This Trap

1. **Be honest about what you really knew.** If you didn't predict something, admit it—don't trick yourself into thinking you did!
2. **Remember that some things are impossible to know.** No one can predict the future 100% of the time.
3. **Learn from what happened.** Instead of saying, *"I knew it,"* ask, *"What can I learn for next time?"*

Try It Yourself!

Imagine you flip a coin. Before flipping, you guess **heads**. It lands on **tails.**
- **Hindsight Bias says:** *"I knew it was going to be tails!"* (But you didn't—you just wish you had guessed differently.)
- **Smart thinking says:** *"I couldn't have known—it was a 50/50 chance."*

How to Think Smarter

Hindsight Bias **makes you believe you "knew" something after it already happened.** But real learning happens when you admit what you **didn't know** and use that knowledge to make **better choices next time.** Instead of saying, *"I knew it all along,"* start asking, *"What can I learn from this?"*

Chapter 22: Groupthink – When Everyone Just Follows the Crowd

Have you ever been in a group where everyone **agrees on something**, even if it doesn't seem like the best idea? Maybe your friends all decide to play a game you don't like, but you go along with it because **you don't want to be the only one who disagrees.**

That's called **Groupthink**—a thinking trap where people **just follow the group instead of thinking for themselves.**

How Groupthink Tricks You

Your brain **wants to fit in.** It doesn't like feeling **left out** or being the only one with a different opinion. So instead of saying, *"I don't think this is a good idea,"* your brain says, *"Just go along with it so no one gets upset."*

Here's how this trap works:

- **Everyone in your class likes a new movie, but you don't.** You pretend to like it so you don't feel different.

- **Your friends want to skip practice, even though you know you should go.** You don't say anything because you don't want to be the only one who disagrees.
- **A group is making a bad choice, but no one speaks up.** Everyone assumes, *"If no one else is saying anything, it must be fine."*

Why This Can Be a Problem

Groupthink can lead to **bad decisions** because no one stops to ask, *"Is this really a good idea?"* It can make you:

- **Do things you wouldn't normally do.**
- **Ignore your own opinions because you're afraid to be different.**
- **Miss out on making better choices.**

How to Avoid This Trap

1. **Ask yourself, "Do I really agree, or am I just going along with the group?"**
2. **Speak up if something doesn't feel right.** Others might be thinking the same thing but are also afraid to say it!
3. **Remember, it's okay to have a different opinion.** Being part of a group **doesn't** mean you have to agree with everything.

Try It Yourself!

Imagine your friends want to sneak snacks into the movies, but you know it's against the rules.

- **Groupthink says:** *"Everyone else is doing it, so I should too."*
- **Smart thinking says:** *"Just because they're doing it doesn't mean I have to."*

The Power of Thinking for Yourself

Groupthink **makes people follow the crowd without thinking.** But **great decision-makers aren't afraid to think for themselves!** Next time you feel pressured to go along with something, **pause and ask yourself if it's really the best choice.** Sometimes, the smartest person in the room is the one who speaks up!

Chapter 23: The Dunning-Kruger Effect – Thinking You're a Genius (When You're Not)

Have you ever met someone who **thinks they're an expert at something—but really isn't?** Maybe a friend brags about being great at a video game, but when they play, they lose **every round.** Or maybe someone claims they "know everything" about a subject but gets a lot of facts wrong.

That's called the **Dunning-Kruger Effect**—a thinking trap where **people who don't know much about something believe they know a lot.**

How the Dunning-Kruger Effect Tricks You

When people learn **a little** about a topic, they sometimes feel **overconfident**—because they don't know enough to realize how much they're actually missing!

Here's how this works:

1. **You try something new and do okay at first.** (*This is easy! I must be great at this!*)
2. **You feel super confident, even though you don't know much yet.** (*I already know enough—I don't need to learn more!*)
3. **Later, you realize it's harder than you thought.** (*Oh... maybe I didn't know as much as I thought!*)

Why This Can Be a Problem

The Dunning-Kruger Effect **tricks you into thinking you're better at something than you really are.** This can lead to:

- Skipping practice because you think you don't need it.
- Not listening to advice from people who actually know more.
- Making mistakes because you didn't take time to learn properly.

How to Avoid This Trap

1. **Ask yourself, "Do I really know enough, or should I learn more?"** If you've only just started something, there's probably **a lot more to learn!**
2. **Listen to experts.** If someone with more experience gives advice, **pay attention instead of assuming you already know best.**
3. **Keep practicing.** The best way to improve is to **keep learning, even if you think you're already good.**

Try It Yourself!

Imagine you've played a game **a few times** and think you're amazing at it. But then you play against an expert and **lose quickly.**

- **Dunning-Kruger Effect says:** *"That was just bad luck. I'm still really good."*
- **Smart thinking says:** *"Maybe I have more to learn! I should watch how they play and improve."*

The Best Way to Get Smarter

The Dunning-Kruger Effect **makes people think they know more than they do.** But truly smart people **always keep learning!** The next time you feel like an expert at something, **ask yourself if there's more to discover.** The more you learn, the better you'll really be!

Part IV: Decision-Making Tools for Kids

Making smart choices isn't just about avoiding thinking traps—it's also about using the **right tools to help you decide.** Just like a builder needs a hammer and a scientist needs a microscope, **great decision-makers use special thinking tools** to make the best choices. In this section, you'll learn **simple and powerful tricks** that can help you **solve problems, compare options, and make better decisions—every time!** Let's start with the **Decision Tree,** a tool that helps you see **where your choices might lead!**

Chapter 24: The Decision Tree – How to Plan Your Choices Step-by-Step

Imagine you're in a maze. At every turn, you have two paths to choose from. Some paths lead to **treasure**, and others lead to **dead ends**. If you could see the whole maze **before you started**, wouldn't it be easier to find the best way through?

That's exactly what a **Decision Tree** does! It helps you **see your choices, think about what might happen, and pick the smartest path.**

How a Decision Tree Works

A Decision Tree is like a map for your choices. Instead of guessing, you write down your options and what could happen next.

Here's how to make one:
1. **Start with your decision.** What are you trying to choose? (*Example: Should I spend my money or save it?*)
2. **Write your options.** List the choices you have. (*Spend it now or save it?*)
3. **Think ahead.** For each choice, write what could happen next. (*If I spend it, I get something now but might regret it later. If I save it, I can buy something even better later!*)
4. **Pick the best path.** Look at your options and choose the one that leads to the best result!

Let's Try It!

Imagine you're deciding whether to **do your homework now or later.**

- **Choice 1: Do it now.** → You finish early → You have free time later with no stress!
- **Choice 2: Do it later.** → You feel rushed before bedtime → You're tired and don't do your best work.

Looking at the Decision Tree, **doing homework now is clearly the better choice!**

Why This Works

Using a Decision Tree helps you:
- **See the future before making a choice.**
- **Avoid bad decisions that lead to problems.**
- **Pick the smartest path instead of guessing.**

A Smart Way to Make Decisions

Next time you have a tricky choice, **draw a Decision Tree!** When you see where each path leads, it's much easier to **make the best decision — and avoid dead ends!**

Chapter 25: The Six Thinking Hats – Seeing a Problem in Different Ways

Imagine you're trying to solve a problem, but everyone in the room has **a different opinion.** One person is **excited**, another is **worried**, someone else is **super logical**, and another just **wants to be creative.** How do you **figure out the best decision** when everyone thinks differently?

That's where the **Six Thinking Hats** method comes in! It's a fun and simple way to **look at a decision from different angles** so you can see the **full picture** before choosing.

What Are the Six Thinking Hats?

Each **Thinking Hat** represents a different way of thinking. When making a decision, you can **"wear" each hat one at a time** to consider all sides.

- **Yellow Hat (Positives)** – What's good about this idea? What are the benefits?
- **Black Hat (Negatives)** – What could go wrong? Are there any risks?
- **Blue Hat (Planning)** – What steps do we need to take to make this work?
- **Red Hat (Feelings)** – How do I feel about this? What does my gut say?
- **Green Hat (Creativity)** – Can I think of a new or different way to do this?
- **White Hat (Facts & Information)** – What do I know? What are the facts?

Let's Try It!

Imagine you're trying to decide whether to **start a lemonade stand.** Let's "wear" each hat and see what it tells us!

- **Yellow Hat:** I could make money and learn how to run a business!
- **Black Hat:** What if no one buys my lemonade? I could lose money.
- **Blue Hat:** I'll need lemons, cups, a table, and a sign to get started.
- **Red Hat:** I feel excited, but a little nervous too!
- **Green Hat:** Maybe I could sell cookies too to attract more customers!
- **White Hat:** It's summer, and people like cold drinks—so it's a good time to try!

By using **all six hats**, you get a **clearer picture** of what might happen instead of only looking at it one way.

Why This Works

The Six Thinking Hats help you:

- **Consider different perspectives before deciding.**
- **Spot problems before they happen.**
- **Find creative solutions instead of only seeing obstacles.**

A Fun Way to Make Better Decisions

Next time you're making a big choice, **try using the Six Thinking Hats!** Looking at a decision from every angle helps you **see things clearly—and make the smartest choice!**

Chapter 26: SWOT Analysis – Strengths, Weaknesses, Opportunities, and Threats

Imagine you're deciding whether to **try out for the school play.** You love acting, but you're also a little nervous. How do you figure out if it's the right choice?

A **SWOT Analysis** is a tool that helps you **weigh the good and bad** before making a decision. It stands for:

- **Strengths** – What are you good at? What will help you succeed?
- **Weaknesses** – What might be hard for you? What could hold you back?
- **Opportunities** – What good things could come from this choice?
- **Threats** – What challenges or risks should you watch out for?

How to Use a SWOT Analysis

A SWOT Analysis helps you **think through a decision step by step** instead of just guessing.

Let's try it with the school play example.

- **Strengths:** You love performing, you're creative, and you remember lines easily.
- **Weaknesses:** You get nervous in front of big crowds, and you've never acted on stage before.
- **Opportunities:** You could make new friends, learn new skills, and gain confidence.
- **Threats:** The play might take up a lot of time, and you might not get the role you want.

By looking at all four areas, you can **see the big picture** and make a **better choice.**

Why This Works

A SWOT Analysis helps you:

- **Understand your strengths and weaknesses before making a decision.**
- **See both the risks and the rewards.**
- **Make a choice based on facts instead of just feelings.**

Try It Yourself!

Imagine you're deciding whether to **join the soccer team.** Before saying yes or no, write down your:

- **Strengths** – Are you fast? Do you enjoy teamwork?
- **Weaknesses** – Do you get tired quickly? Are you new to the sport?
- **Opportunities** – Will you learn new skills? Make new friends?
- **Threats** – Will it take too much time? Could you get injured?

A Simple Way to Make Smarter Choices

The next time you have a big decision, **use a SWOT Analysis!** It helps you see **both the good and the bad** so you can choose wisely and feel **confident** in your decision!

Chapter 27: Pro/Con Lists Done Right – Why Writing It Down Helps

Factor	Pro/Con	Weight	Impact	Score
Go to sleepover	Pro	9	+8	+72
Be popular with friends	Pro	8	+7	+56
Might not sleep well	Con	7	-6	-42
Far from family	Con	6	-5	-30

Pros Total: +128   Cons Total: -72   Net Score: +56

Have you ever had **two choices** and felt stuck on which one to pick? Maybe you're trying to decide whether to **go to a sleepover or stay home for a family movie night.** Both sound fun, so how do you choose?

A **Pro/Con List** is a simple way to **see the good and bad of each option** by writing them down. When you see your choices clearly, making a decision becomes **much easier!**

How to Make a Pro/Con List

A **Pro** is something **good** about a choice.

A **Con** is something **not so good** about it.

Let's say you're deciding whether to go to the sleepover or stay home.

Option 1: Go to the Sleepover
Pros:
- You get to hang out with friends.
- You'll have fun playing games and watching movies.
- You might make great memories.

Cons:
- You might not sleep well.
- You could miss your family's movie night.
- You have an early soccer game the next morning.

Option 2: Stay Home for Family Movie Night
Pros:
- You'll be well-rested for soccer.
- You get to spend time with family.
- You don't have to pack an overnight bag.

Cons:
- You'll miss the fun with friends.
- You might feel left out if they talk about it later.

Why This Works

A Pro/Con List helps you:

- **See your choices clearly instead of just guessing.**
- **Think about what really matters most.**
- **Make a smart decision you'll be happy with later.**

Try It Yourself!

The next time you're stuck between two choices, grab a piece of paper and **write down the pros and cons.** You might be surprised at how **much easier** your decision becomes!

A Simple Trick for Smarter Decisions

Sometimes, a choice feels difficult just because you haven't **seen it on paper.** Writing down the pros and cons helps you **stop overthinking and start deciding.** Try it next time, and see how much clearer your choices become!

Chapter 28: Scenario Planning – Imagining What Could Go Right (or Wrong)

Have you ever made a choice and later thought, **"I didn't expect that to happen!"**? Maybe you went outside without a jacket because it looked sunny, but then it started raining. Or maybe you picked a hard level in a game without checking what you needed, and you lost right away.

That's where **Scenario Planning** helps! It's a decision-making tool that lets you **think ahead and imagine different outcomes** before making a choice.

How Scenario Planning Works

Instead of just picking something and hoping for the best, **Scenario Planning helps you ask, "What could happen next?"**

Here's how to do it:
1. **Think about your decision.** What are you trying to choose? (*Example: Should I bring an umbrella today?*)
2. **Imagine different scenarios.** What are the possible outcomes? (*It might stay sunny, or it could rain.*)
3. **Decide what's smartest based on the possibilities.** (*Since rain is possible, it's better to bring an umbrella just in case!*)

Let's Try It!

Imagine you're deciding whether to **ride your bike to school or take the bus.**

- **Scenario 1:** You ride your bike, and the weather stays nice. *Great choice!*
- **Scenario 2:** You ride your bike, but it starts raining. *Now you're wet and uncomfortable!*
- **Scenario 3:** You take the bus, and it turns out to be a super hot day. *You avoided sweating on your bike ride!*

After thinking through the scenarios, you **might decide to check the weather before choosing.**

Why This Works

Scenario Planning helps you:
- **Avoid surprises by thinking ahead.**
- **Make smarter choices based on different possibilities.**
- **Be prepared for whatever happens!**

Try It Yourself!

The next time you have a decision to make, ask yourself:
- *What are the different things that could happen?*
- *Will I still be happy with my choice in each situation?*
- *How can I prepare for the best and worst outcomes?*

A Clever Way to Avoid Surprises

Scenario Planning **helps you think ahead instead of guessing.** The more you practice imagining different outcomes, the better you'll be at making choices that **work out well — no matter what happens!**

Chapter 29: Pre-Mortem Analysis – Thinking About Failing Before It Happens

Have you ever started something **only to realize later that you made a big mistake**? Maybe you forgot to bring supplies for a school project, or you started a game without checking the rules and lost quickly.

Wouldn't it be great if you could **spot mistakes before they happen?** That's exactly what **Pre-Mortem Analysis** helps you do! It's a simple way to **imagine what could go wrong before you make a decision** so you can fix problems before they happen.

How Pre-Mortem Analysis Works

Instead of only thinking, *What if this goes well?*, you also ask, *What if this goes wrong?* Then, you figure out how to **avoid those problems before they happen.**

Here's how to do it:

1. **Imagine you made your decision—and it completely failed.** What went wrong?
2. **List all the possible reasons for the failure.** Did you forget something? Did you not prepare enough?
3. **Make a plan to prevent those mistakes.** Now that you know what could go wrong, you can fix it before it happens!

Let's Try It!

Imagine you are about to **give a class presentation.** Instead of just hoping it goes well, you do a Pre-Mortem Analysis.

- **Possible failure:** You forget what to say in the middle of the presentation.
- **Solution:** Practice in front of a mirror or with a friend so you feel more confident.
- **Possible failure:** The slideshow doesn't work.
- **Solution:** Print out notes so you can continue even if the screen doesn't load.

By thinking ahead, you **catch problems before they happen** and have a plan to handle them!

Why This Works

Pre-Mortem Analysis helps you:

- **Prepare for problems instead of being surprised by them.**
- **Feel more confident because you're ready for anything.**
- **Make smarter choices by avoiding mistakes before they happen.**

A Smart Way to Stay One Step Ahead

The next time you make a big decision, **imagine what could go wrong first.** When you plan for problems before they happen, you'll always be **one step ahead—and ready to succeed!**

Chapter 30: Heuristic Shortcuts – Quick Thinking, but Smarter

Have you ever **made a quick decision without really thinking about it?** Maybe you always pick the same snack at lunch because you know you like it. Or maybe you guessed the answer on a test because it "felt right."

Your brain **likes to save time**, so it uses **shortcuts** to help you make choices quickly. These shortcuts are called **heuristics**—they help you **think fast**, but sometimes they can **lead you in the wrong direction.**

How Heuristic Shortcuts Work

Your brain takes **shortcuts** so you don't have to stop and think about every little thing.

Here are some common shortcuts:

- **The Familiarity Shortcut** – You pick something just because you know it. (*Example: You always choose pepperoni pizza because it's what you usually eat—even though another flavor might be great!*)

- **The Popularity Shortcut** – You assume something is good just because lots of people like it. (*Example: Everyone at school is wearing a certain brand of shoes, so you think you need them too.*)
- **The First Answer Shortcut** – You believe the first thing you hear. (*Example: Your friend tells you a new kid is mean, so you believe it without getting to know them yourself.*)

When Heuristics Help

Sometimes, heuristics make life **easier and faster.**
- **Choosing clothes in the morning** – You don't need to try on everything in your closet.
- **Finding your favorite cereal at the store** – You grab it without reading every box.
- **Staying safe** – If something looks dangerous, you move away fast instead of stopping to think.

When Heuristics Cause Mistakes

But **fast thinking isn't always smart thinking.**
- **You assume a game will be fun** just because the cover looks cool.
- **You think you know the answer on a test** without reading the question carefully.
- **You believe a rumor** because you heard it from one person instead of checking if it's true.

How to Use Heuristics Wisely

1. **Pause before making a fast decision.** Ask yourself, *Am I choosing this just because it's easy?*
2. **Check the facts.** If something sounds unbelievable, make sure it's true before you believe it.
3. **Trust shortcuts only when they make sense.** If a decision is important, **slow down and think it through.**

Try It Yourself!

Imagine your friend tells you a **new movie is boring** before you even see it.

- **Fast thinking says:** "I won't watch it—it must be bad!"
- **Smart thinking says:** "Maybe I should see it for myself before deciding!"

How to Think Fast Without Making Mistakes

Heuristics help you **make quick choices**, but they can also **lead you the wrong way.** The key is to **know when to trust them—and when to slow down and think.** Smart decision-makers **use shortcuts wisely** instead of letting shortcuts **control their thinking!**

Part V: Emotions and Decision-Making

Making choices isn't just about **thinking logically**—your **feelings** play a big role too! Sometimes, emotions **help you make good decisions**, like feeling excited about trying something new. But other times, emotions can **push you into bad choices**, like saying something mean when you're angry. In this section, you'll learn how to **balance your feelings with smart thinking** so you can make decisions that you won't regret later!

Chapter 31: Self-Regulation – Keeping Your Feelings in Check

Have you ever **said or done something you regretted** just because you were mad, sad, or frustrated? Maybe you **shouted at a friend** when you were upset or **quit a game** because you lost. Later, you probably thought, *I wish I had handled that better!*

That's where **self-regulation** comes in. It means **controlling your emotions instead of letting them control you.** It helps you **stay calm, think clearly, and make better choices — even when you're feeling strong emotions.**

How Emotions Can Lead to Bad Choices

When emotions take over, **it's easy to make mistakes.**

- **Anger:** You snap at a friend without thinking, then feel bad later.
- **Fear:** You don't try something new because you're scared you'll fail.

- **Excitement:** You rush into a decision without thinking about the consequences.

How to Stay in Control

Instead of letting emotions **push you into bad choices**, use these simple tricks to stay in control:

1. **Pause before reacting.** If you feel a strong emotion, **take a deep breath** and give yourself a few seconds to think.
2. **Name your feeling.** Say to yourself, *I'm feeling angry* or *I'm feeling nervous.* Just recognizing your emotion can help you handle it better.
3. **Ask yourself, "What happens next?"** Think about what will happen if you act on your emotion. Will you regret it?
4. **Find a way to calm down.** If you're too upset to think clearly, try taking a walk, listening to music, or counting to ten.

Try It Yourself!

Imagine your little brother **takes your favorite toy without asking.**

- **Reacting without control:** You yell and grab it back, making him cry.
- **Using self-regulation:** You take a deep breath and calmly tell him, *Please ask next time.*

Why This Matters

Self-regulation **helps you make better decisions, avoid regrets, and handle tough situations with confidence.** The more you practice it, the easier it gets! Instead of letting your emotions **take over**, you'll learn to **stay in control and choose wisely.**

Chapter 32: Empathy and Decisions – Thinking About Others Before You Choose

Have you ever made a decision that seemed good for you—but later realized it **hurt someone else**? Maybe you **grabbed the last piece of cake** without asking if anyone else wanted it, or you **chose a game that you liked** but your friend didn't enjoy.

That's where **empathy** comes in. Empathy means **understanding how someone else feels.** It helps you make decisions that aren't just good for you—but also **kind and fair to others.**

How Empathy Helps You Make Better Choices

Before making a decision, empathy helps you **stop and think about how it affects others.**

Let's say you're deciding whether to:

- **Take the biggest cookie for yourself.** (*How will that make others feel?*)
- **Interrupt a friend while they're talking.** (*Would I like it if someone did that to me?*)
- **Leave someone out of a game.** (*How would I feel if I were them?*)

By thinking about how your actions **affect others**, you can **make better choices that keep everyone happy.**

How to Use Empathy in Your Decisions

Before making a choice, ask yourself:

1. **How would I feel if this happened to me?**
2. **Will my choice hurt someone else's feelings?**
3. **Is there a way to make a fairer decision?**

Try It Yourself!

Imagine your friend really wants to play a board game, but you want to play video games instead.

- **Without empathy:** You ignore their idea and play what you want.
- **With empathy:** You take turns so both of you get to play what you enjoy.

Why This Matters

Empathy **helps you be a better friend, teammate, and family member.** It makes sure that your choices **aren't just good for you, but also fair and kind to others.** When you use empathy in decision-making, **everyone wins!**

Chapter 33: The Role of Intuition – When Your Gut Feeling Is (or Isn't) Right

Have you ever had a feeling deep inside that told you what to do—even when you weren't sure why? Maybe you met someone new and instantly felt like you could trust them, or you got a weird feeling about a situation and decided to walk away.

That feeling is called **intuition**, or your **gut feeling**. It's like a little voice in your head that **helps you make quick decisions** without thinking too hard. But here's the trick—sometimes your gut is **right**, and sometimes it **leads you the wrong way!**

When You Should Trust Your Gut

Intuition works best when your brain **recognizes patterns** from past experiences.

You can trust your gut when:
- **You've practiced something a lot.** If you've played soccer for years, your gut will often help you make quick moves without thinking.
- **You sense danger.** If a situation **feels wrong**, your brain might be picking up on something you don't fully understand.
- **You're making a simple decision.** If you're picking between two ice cream flavors, your gut can quickly tell you which one you like more!

When Your Gut Might Be Wrong

Intuition isn't always right, especially when:
- **You're in a new situation.** Your gut can't guide you well if you've never been in this situation before.
- **Emotions are controlling your decision.** If you're **angry, scared, or too excited**, your gut might push you to make a bad choice.
- **You're making a big, important decision.** Choosing a school, spending money, or making a big commitment **needs more than just a gut feeling—you need to think it through!**

How to Use Intuition the Smart Way

Before trusting your gut, ask yourself:
1. **Have I been in this situation before?** (*If yes, my gut might be right! If no, I should think more before deciding.*)
2. **Am I feeling emotional right now?** (*If I'm upset, I should slow down and think instead of rushing my decision.*)
3. **Is this a big decision?** (*For big choices, I should gather facts and not just rely on my feelings.*)

Try It Yourself!

Imagine your friends want to explore a shortcut through the woods, but something **feels off** about it.
- **Listening to your gut:** You decide not to go because your gut tells you it might not be safe. Later, you find out it was full of poison ivy!

- **Not listening to your gut:** You ignore the weird feeling and go anyway, ending up itchy for days.

The Right Way to Trust Your Gut

Intuition **can be a powerful tool, but it's not always right.** The best decision-makers know when to **listen to their gut — and when to slow down and think things through.** The next time you have a gut feeling, **pause and check if it's leading you in the right direction!**

Chapter 34: Dealing with Decision Fatigue – Why Too Many Choices Make You Tired

Have you ever felt so **tired of making decisions** that you just **pick anything to get it over with**? Maybe you spent all day choosing what to wear, what to eat, what game to play, and then by the end of the day, when someone asks, *"What do you want for dinner?"* you just say, **"I don't care!"**

That's called **Decision Fatigue**—when your brain gets **tired from making too many choices**, and you start making **lazy or bad decisions** just because you don't want to think anymore.

Why Too Many Choices Make You Tired

Your brain **uses energy every time you make a decision**—even for small things like picking a snack or choosing a song. The more choices you make in a day, the **more tired your brain gets.**

Here's what happens when Decision Fatigue kicks in:
- **You make random choices** just to get it over with. (*Example: You grab the first snack you see instead of picking something healthy.*)
- **You avoid making a choice at all.** (*Example: You can't decide what to watch, so you just sit there doing nothing.*)
- **You go for the easiest option—even if it's not the best.** (*Example: You pick a book for a school project that you don't even like, just because you don't want to think anymore.*)

How to Beat Decision Fatigue

Instead of letting your brain get **tired and overwhelmed**, use these tricks to make choices **easier**:

1. **Make fewer decisions.** If you don't have to choose, don't! (*Example: Wear the same favorite outfit each Monday so you don't have to think about it!*)
2. **Decide important things early.** If you wait until you're tired, you'll make worse choices. (*Example: Pack your lunch the night before instead of deciding in the morning when you're sleepy.*)
3. **Use routines.** If you do something the same way every time, your brain doesn't have to think about it. (*Example: Always do homework right after school so you don't have to decide when to start.*)

Try It Yourself!

Imagine you're picking a movie to watch.
- **With Decision Fatigue:** You scroll for 30 minutes, feel exhausted, and pick something random you don't even like.
- **Without Decision Fatigue:** You make a list of your favorite movies **beforehand**, so next time, you just choose from your list in seconds!

A Fun and Easy Way to Make Good Decisions

The more choices you make in a day, **the harder it gets to make good ones.** The trick to avoiding Decision Fatigue is to **simplify your choices, plan ahead, and use routines** so your brain doesn't get too tired. When you **save your energy for the big decisions,** you'll make **better choices all day long!**

Chapter 35: Stress-Reduction Techniques – How to Stay Calm Under Pressure

Have you ever felt **so stressed** about making a decision that you just **froze** and couldn't decide at all? Maybe you had to pick a topic for a school project, but you felt overwhelmed by all the options. Or maybe you had to decide which team to join, and the pressure made you nervous.

When you're **stressed out**, it's **harder to think clearly**—and that can lead to bad decisions. That's why learning **how to stay calm** can help you make **better choices, even in tough situations.**

Why Stress Makes Decision-Making Harder

When you feel stressed, your brain **goes into panic mode.** Instead of thinking things through, you might:

- **Rush into a decision** just to get it over with. (*Example: Picking a random science project instead of one you actually like.*)
- **Avoid deciding at all** because it feels too overwhelming. (*Example: Not choosing a summer activity and missing the deadline to sign up!*)
- **Make choices based on fear** instead of logic. (*Example: Skipping a big opportunity because you're afraid of failing.*)

How to Stay Calm and Make Better Choices

Instead of letting stress take over, try these simple tricks to **calm your brain before making a decision:**

1. **Take a deep breath.** When you're stressed, your brain speeds up. Taking a deep breath helps you **slow down and think clearly.**
2. **Break big decisions into small steps.** Instead of thinking *"I have to decide everything right now,"* start with the **first step** and go from there.
3. **Ask for help.** Sometimes talking to a friend, parent, or teacher can **help you see your choices more clearly.**
4. **Take a short break.** If a decision is making you **too stressed**, step away for a few minutes. A quick walk or listening to music can help clear your mind.
5. **Remind yourself that no decision is perfect.** You don't have to make the *perfect* choice—just the best one for you at the moment.

Try It Yourself!

Imagine you're feeling **stressed about picking a club to join at school.**

- **Without stress control:** You panic, pick the first club you see, and later realize it's not what you wanted.
- **With stress control:** You take a deep breath, look at your options, and **choose the club that fits your interests best.**

How to Make Choices Without Feeling Stuck

Stress can make decision-making feel **overwhelming,** but the trick is to **slow down, breathe, and take small steps.** When you **stay calm, you think more clearly**—and that helps you make **better choices, no matter the situation!**

Chapter 36: The Pause Principle – Stop, Breathe, and Think Before You Act

Have you ever **answered too quickly** and then realized you said the wrong thing? Or agreed to something **before thinking it through** and later wished you had chosen differently?

That's why the **Pause Principle** is so important! It's a simple trick that helps you **stop, think, and make a better choice**—instead of rushing into a decision you might regret.

Why Rushing Leads to Bad Decisions

Your brain **wants to decide fast**, but quick choices aren't always smart ones.

- **You say "yes" to something you don't want to do** just because you feel pressured.
- **You send a text when you're mad** and regret it later.
- **You pick the first answer on a test** without reading the question carefully.

How the Pause Principle Works

Before making a decision, **pause for a moment** and ask yourself:

1. **Do I really want to do this?** (*Or am I just saying yes because I feel pressured?*)
2. **Will I regret this choice later?** (*If I take a second to think, will I pick something better?*)
3. **What happens next?** (*If I say this, do this, or choose this, how will it affect me?*)

Try It Yourself!

Imagine your friend **dares you to do something silly in front of a big crowd.**

- **Without pausing:** You say yes immediately, but later feel embarrassed.
- **With the Pause Principle:** You stop and think, *Do I actually want to do this?* You decide to say no and feel much better about your choice.

Why This Works

The Pause Principle helps you:

- Avoid bad decisions that come from pressure or emotions.
- Think before you act, so you don't regret your choice later.
- Feel more confident about the decisions you make.

A Simple Trick to Make Smarter Choices

Next time you're about to **make a quick decision**, stop for a second. **That tiny pause can help you avoid mistakes, stay in control, and make choices you'll feel good about later!**

Chapter 37: Handling Regret – Learning from Mistakes Without Feeling Bad Forever

Have you ever made a decision and later thought, **"I wish I had chosen differently"**? Maybe you spent all your money on a toy and then saw something even cooler the next day. Or maybe you said something unkind in an argument and felt bad afterward.

That feeling is called **regret**—and everyone experiences it sometimes. The good news? **Regret can actually help you make better choices in the future—if you handle it the right way!**

Why Do People Feel Regret?

Regret happens when you realize:

- **You made a choice too quickly.** (*Example: You rushed to pick a snack and later wished you had chosen something better.*)

- **You ignored your gut feeling.** (*Example: You felt unsure about skipping practice but did it anyway—and later regretted it.*)
- **You acted on emotions instead of thinking it through.** (*Example: You yelled at a friend and later wished you had stayed calm.*)

What to Do When You Feel Regret

Instead of feeling **stuck** in regret, use it as a chance to **learn and grow.**

1. **Accept that everyone makes mistakes.** Even the smartest people in the world make choices they later regret.
2. **Ask yourself, "What can I learn from this?"** If you regret something, think about how you can make a better choice next time.
3. **Apologize if you need to.** If your decision hurt someone else, saying sorry can **help fix the situation** and make you both feel better.
4. **Move forward.** Regret is only helpful if you use it to make better choices. Once you've learned your lesson, let it go and focus on what's next!

Try It Yourself!

Imagine you **forgot to study for a test and got a bad grade.**

- **Feeling stuck in regret:** You keep thinking, *I'm terrible at this. I should have studied!* but don't do anything to change it.
- **Using regret to grow:** You say, *Next time, I'll plan ahead and study a little each day!*

How to Turn Regret into a Lesson

Regret **doesn't have to be a bad thing**—it can actually **make you a smarter decision-maker!** The next time you make a mistake, don't just feel bad about it. **Ask yourself what you can learn, make a plan to do better, and move forward with confidence!**

Chapter 38: Making Peace with Uncertainty – Accepting That You Can't Know Everything

Have you ever had to make a decision but **felt unsure** because you didn't have all the answers? Maybe you were picking a new activity to try but weren't sure if you'd like it. Or maybe you were deciding whether to introduce yourself to someone new but didn't know how they would react.

That feeling of **not knowing everything** is called **uncertainty**—and it's completely normal! No one can predict the future, but that doesn't mean you should avoid making decisions. Learning to **make peace with uncertainty** helps you **move forward with confidence, even when you don't have all the answers.**

Why Uncertainty Feels Uncomfortable

Your brain **likes knowing things for sure**, so when there are unknowns, you might feel:

- **Worried about making the wrong choice.** (*What if I pick the wrong activity and don't like it?*)
- **Afraid of failure.** (*What if I try and don't do well?*)
- **Stuck and unable to decide.** (*Maybe I just won't choose at all!*)

But here's the truth: **Most great decisions happen even when you don't know everything!**

How to Make Good Decisions Even When You're Unsure

Instead of waiting until you have **every single answer**, try these strategies:

1. **Gather what information you can.** (*Example: If you're picking a club to join, ask someone who's already in it what it's like!*)
2. **Accept that some things are unknown.** (*Example: You won't know if you love a new activity until you try it—and that's okay!*)
3. **Take a small step instead of a big leap.** (*Example: If you're unsure about a new hobby, try it once before fully committing!*)

Try It Yourself!

Imagine you're deciding **whether to enter a competition.**

- **Getting stuck in uncertainty:** You think, *What if I'm not good enough? What if I don't win?* So, you decide not to try at all.
- **Making peace with uncertainty:** You think, *I don't know what will happen, but I can try my best and learn from the experience.*

Why It's Okay Not to Know Everything

No one can predict the future, but that shouldn't stop you from making decisions. Instead of feeling stuck, **accept that some things are unknown**—and make the best choice you can with what you do know! The more you practice, the easier it gets to **trust yourself, even when things feel uncertain.**

Part VI: Making Decisions with Others

Not every decision is just about **you** — sometimes, you have to make choices **with other people.** Whether it's deciding what game to play with friends, working on a school project, or solving a disagreement, learning how to **listen, share ideas, and work as a team** is super important. In this section, you'll learn how to **make group decisions that are fair, smart, and keep everyone happy!**

Part VI: Making Decisions with Options

Chapter 39: Consensus-Building – Getting a Group to Agree

Have you ever been in a group where **no one could agree on what to do?** Maybe one friend wanted to play soccer, another wanted to play tag, and someone else wanted to just sit and talk. How do you make a decision that **everyone** feels good about?

That's where **consensus-building** comes in! It's a way of making decisions where **everyone shares their ideas, listens to each other, and works together to find the best choice.** Instead of one person deciding for the whole group, **everyone gets a say.**

How Consensus-Building Works

Instead of arguing or just doing what the loudest person wants, you follow these simple steps:
1. **Listen to everyone's ideas.** Each person shares what they think, and everyone listens without interrupting.

2. **Find common ground.** Look for something **most people agree on.**
3. **Talk through the options.** If people disagree, see if there's a way to **combine ideas** or find a middle ground.
4. **Make a final decision that feels fair.** Everyone might not get exactly what they want, but **no one should feel ignored or left out.**

Let's Try It!

Imagine your group is trying to **pick a movie for a sleepover.**

- **One person wants a funny movie.**
- **Another wants an action movie.**
- **Someone else wants a cartoon.**

Instead of arguing, you could:

- Find a movie that has both action and comedy.
- Take a vote and let the group decide.
- Plan to watch one type of movie this time and a different one next time.

Now, instead of **one person being unhappy,** everyone feels included!

Why This Works

Consensus-building helps you:

- **Make group decisions without arguing.**
- **Make sure everyone's voice is heard.**
- **Find solutions that work for everyone, not just one person.**

How to Make Group Decisions Without Fighting

The next time you and your friends or family **can't agree on something**, try using consensus-building. **When everyone feels included in the decision, people are happier, and things go much more smoothly!**

Chapter 40: Avoiding Power Dynamics – When Someone Bossy Takes Over

Have you ever been in a group where **one person made all the decisions** without listening to anyone else? Maybe a bossy friend chose the game without asking what others wanted. Or maybe a loud classmate took over a group project while everyone else just followed along.

This is called a **power dynamic** — when one person has **more control over a decision than everyone else.** It can make choices feel **unfair** and leave others feeling ignored. But good decision-making means **everyone's voice should count!**

Why Power Dynamics Can Be a Problem

When one person takes over, group decisions can go wrong:

- **Some people feel left out.** (*Example: A leader picks the game, but half the group doesn't want to play.*)

- **Others just go along with it, even if they don't agree.** (*Example: A classmate makes all the decisions for a project, but no one else speaks up.*)
- **It's not really a fair choice.** (*Example: A coach always picks the same players first, even if others deserve a turn.*)

How to Make Sure Everyone's Voice Counts

Instead of letting **one person** control the decision, try these fair ways to decide:

1. **Take turns leading.** If your group makes decisions often, let a different person lead each time.
2. **Use voting.** If there are two or three choices, let everyone vote so the majority decides.
3. **Ask for opinions.** Before deciding, go around the group and let everyone share their thoughts.
4. **Make sure quiet people get a chance to speak.** Some people don't like to talk over others, so check in with them.

Try It Yourself!

Imagine your friend group is picking a game, but one person **always chooses what they want** without asking anyone else.

- **With power dynamics:** That person picks, and others don't get a say.
- **Without power dynamics:** Everyone suggests a game, and the group votes or takes turns choosing.

How to Make Group Decisions Fair for Everyone

A good group decision **doesn't let one person take over**—it makes sure **everyone gets a voice.** The next time you're making a choice with others, **be fair, listen to everyone, and make sure no one feels ignored!**

Chapter 41: The Wisdom of Crowds – When More People Make a Smarter Choice

Have you ever noticed that **big decisions** are often made by groups instead of just one person? Schools have student councils, governments have teams of leaders, and game shows let the audience help answer tough questions.

That's because of something called **the wisdom of crowds** — the idea that **a group of people, thinking together, often makes a better decision than one person alone.** When different people **share their ideas and knowledge**, the group can **see the full picture and make a smarter choice.**

Why Groups Make Smarter Decisions

No one person **knows everything**, but when people **combine their knowledge**, they can:

- **Catch mistakes that one person might miss.** (*Example: One student might forget part of a project, but another remembers it!*)
- **Come up with more creative ideas.** (*Example: A team brainstorming together can think of better solutions than just one person alone.*)
- **Balance different opinions.** (*Example: If one person wants a risky choice, others might suggest a safer option.*)

When Groups Make Bad Decisions

Groups don't always get it right. Sometimes, they can be **wrong together** if:

- **Everyone copies what others say without thinking for themselves.** (*Example: If one person shouts an answer, others might agree just to fit in—even if it's wrong!*)
- **People don't share their true opinions.** (*Example: Someone might have a great idea but stay quiet because they're nervous.*)
- **The group follows the loudest person instead of listening to all voices.**

How to Use the Wisdom of Crowds the Right Way

To make good group decisions, follow these steps:

1. **Get different opinions.** Ask people with different experiences and ideas to share their thoughts.
2. **Think for yourself, too.** Just because the group is choosing something doesn't mean it's automatically right—double-check the facts.
3. **Make sure everyone speaks up.** Sometimes, the best ideas come from the quietest voices.

Try It Yourself!

Imagine your class is guessing **how many jellybeans are in a jar.**

- **One person guesses alone:** They might be way off.
- **A whole class guesses together:** By averaging everyone's guesses, the group gets much closer to the right answer!

Why Listening to a Group Can Help You Decide

The **wisdom of crowds** works best when **everyone shares their ideas and listens to each other.** The next time you have a big decision, try **asking a group of people for their opinions—you might end up with a much better choice than you could have made alone!**

Chapter 42: The Delphi Technique – Getting Advice the Right Way

Have you ever been in a group where people **argued so much that no decision was made at all**? Maybe your class tried to pick a field trip location, but everyone shouted their opinions, and nothing got decided. Or maybe your team was choosing a name, but no one could agree because everyone wanted their own idea to win.

That's where **the Delphi Technique** comes in! It's a smart way to **help groups make better decisions** without arguing. Instead of letting the loudest person take over, this method lets **everyone share their ideas in a fair and organized way.**

How the Delphi Technique Works

Instead of **arguing in a big discussion**, the group follows these steps:

1. **Everyone writes down their ideas separately.** This way, no one is influenced by others.

2. **A leader collects the answers and shares them anonymously.** That means no one knows whose idea is whose.
3. **Everyone looks at all the ideas and gives feedback.** The group discusses which ideas are the best and why.
4. **The group votes or revises ideas until they reach the best decision.**

By doing it this way, people **think carefully instead of just going along with the crowd**, and quieter voices get heard too!

Why This Works

The Delphi Technique helps groups:

- **Avoid arguments** by letting people share their ideas in a calmer way.
- **Think deeply** instead of just choosing the first idea that pops up.
- **Make fairer decisions** because no one's opinion is ignored.

Try It Yourself!

Imagine your class is trying to decide **what to do for a school fundraiser.**

- **Without the Delphi Technique:** The loudest students argue, and some kids don't even get a chance to share their ideas.
- **With the Delphi Technique:** Everyone writes their ideas down, all ideas are shared fairly, and the best one is chosen based on what works best for the whole group.

A Better Way to Make Group Decisions

The Delphi Technique **helps groups make decisions without pressure, arguing, or unfairness.** Next time you're in a group that can't agree, suggest **writing down ideas first**—you might be surprised at how much smoother things go!

Chapter 43: Role Assignment – Giving Everyone a Job in Group Decisions

Have you ever been in a group project where **one person did all the work** while others just sat around? Or maybe **everyone tried to lead at the same time**, and it turned into a big mess?

That's why **Role Assignment** is important! It means **giving each person in the group a specific job** so that everything gets done **fairly and efficiently.** When everyone knows their role, the group works together smoothly—and decisions are made without chaos.

Why Role Assignment Helps

When a group doesn't assign roles:

- **Some people do everything, while others do nothing.** (*Example: One student writes the whole project while the rest just watch.*)

- **Everyone tries to be in charge, leading to arguments.** (*Example: Two people try to be the leader, and they keep disagreeing on what to do next.*)
- **Important details get forgotten.** (*Example: The group picks a great idea but forgets to check if it's even possible.*)

When **everyone has a role**, work gets done faster, **everyone feels included**, and decisions are made more easily.

Common Roles in Group Decisions

Depending on the situation, different roles might be needed. Here are a few examples:

1. **The Leader** – Helps keep the group focused and makes sure everyone is included.
2. **The Researcher** – Looks up important facts or information to help make a smart choice.
3. **The Organizer** – Makes a plan for how to get things done step by step.
4. **The Question-Asker** – Challenges ideas by asking, *"Did we think of everything?"*
5. **The Speaker** – Shares the group's decision with others once it's made.

By **dividing responsibilities**, everyone has a part to play, and no one feels left out.

Try It Yourself!

Imagine your class is **planning a talent show.**

- **Without Role Assignment:** Everyone argues about what to do, and no one is sure who is in charge.
- **With Role Assignment:** One person leads, another organizes sign-ups, another handles decorations, and another makes sure all acts are scheduled. Everything runs smoothly!

A Simple Way to Make Group Decisions Work Better

Next time you're in a group, try **assigning roles.** When everyone has a job, **decisions happen faster, work gets done fairly, and the group succeeds as a team!**

Chapter 44: Encouraging Constructive Dissent – Speaking Up When You Disagree

Have you ever been in a group where everyone agreed on something, but you **weren't so sure** it was the best idea? Maybe your friends wanted to take a shortcut on a hike, but you thought it looked unsafe. Or maybe your class picked a project idea that didn't make sense, but no one wanted to say anything.

It can feel uncomfortable to **disagree with a group**, but sometimes **speaking up is the right thing to do.** That's called **constructive dissent**—when you share a different opinion in a way that helps the group **think more carefully and make a better decision.**

Why Speaking Up Matters

When people **never question an idea**, mistakes can happen.

- **A team picks the first idea without thinking it through** – Later, they realize it wasn't the best option.
- **A group follows a risky plan** – No one speaks up, even though someone had doubts.
- **People agree just to fit in** – This is when people go along with something just because they don't want to be different.

How to Disagree the Right Way

Sharing a different opinion **doesn't mean arguing or being rude**—it means **helping the group see other possibilities**. Here's how to do it the right way:

1. **Stay respectful.** Instead of saying, *"That's a bad idea,"* try, *"I see it differently—can I share my thoughts?"*
2. **Explain your reason.** Say why you disagree and give a clear example.
3. **Suggest an alternative.** Instead of just saying no, offer a new idea that might work better.

Try It Yourself!

Imagine your group is **choosing a fundraiser idea**, and they all want to sell something expensive.

- **Staying silent:** You know some people can't afford it, but you don't say anything. The fundraiser doesn't go well.
- **Using constructive dissent:** You say, *"That's a cool idea, but what if we also sell something more affordable so everyone can participate?"* Now, the group has a better plan!

Why Disagreeing Can Lead to Smarter Choices

Speaking up when something **doesn't seem right** can help **prevent mistakes, improve ideas, and make sure everyone is included.** The next time you're in a group, **don't be afraid to share a different perspective—it might just lead to the best decision!**

Chapter 45: Accountability in Groups – Taking Responsibility for Decisions

Have you ever been in a group where **someone didn't do their part**? Maybe your class was working on a poster, but one person forgot their job, and everyone else had to fix it. Or maybe your team was supposed to clean up after an event, but some people left early, and others had to do extra work.

When people don't **take responsibility**, it can lead to frustration, unfinished work, and bad decisions. But when everyone **does their part and owns up to their actions**, the group works better — and things turn out great!

Why Taking Responsibility Matters

When no one takes responsibility, problems happen:

- **Things don't get done.** (*Example: The group plans a bake sale, but no one brings the supplies!*)

- **People get blamed.** (*Example: A mistake happens, but instead of fixing it, everyone just argues about whose fault it was.*)
- **Some people do all the work.** (*Example: A few kids finish a project while others just sit back and watch.*)

But when everyone **does their part**, groups can **make better decisions and work as a real team!**

How to Be Responsible in a Group

1. **Keep your promises.** If you say you'll do something, make sure you actually do it.
2. **Speak up if you make a mistake.** If you forgot something or need help, tell the group so you can fix it together.
3. **Check in with each other.** Ask, *"Does everyone have what they need?"* before it's too late.
4. **Give credit to everyone.** If the group does well, celebrate together instead of letting one person take all the credit.

Try It Yourself!

Imagine your class is working on **a play for school.**

- **Without accountability:** One person forgets their lines but doesn't practice, so the whole scene gets messed up.
- **With accountability:** They admit they need help, and the group helps them rehearse. The play turns out great!

Why Responsibility Makes Teams Stronger

When everyone in a group **takes responsibility**, things get done faster, decisions are fairer, and the whole team **feels proud of their work.** The next time you're in a group, **do your part, be honest, and help each other out—that's how great teams make great choices!**

Part VII: Thinking Ahead for the Future

Making decisions isn't just about **what's happening right now** — some choices affect your future, too! The decisions you make today can shape **what happens tomorrow, next week, or even years from now.** That's why learning to **think ahead** is so important. In this section, you'll discover smart ways to **plan for the future, avoid big mistakes, and make choices that help you succeed in the long run!**

Chapter 46: Game Theory Basics – Making the Best Move in Every Situation

Have you ever played a game where you had to **think ahead to win**? Maybe in chess, you planned your next few moves before making them. Or in tag, you predicted where your friend would run so you could tag them faster.

That's exactly how **Game Theory** works! It's all about **thinking ahead, predicting what others will do, and making the smartest move based on that.**

How Game Theory Works

Game Theory helps you **make better choices** by asking:
1. **What do I want to happen?** (*Example: I want to win this board game.*)
2. **What might the other person do?** (*Example: My opponent will probably block my next move.*)

3. **What's the smartest move based on that?** (*Example: I'll plan two steps ahead so they can't stop me!*)

It's like playing a **strategy game in real life!**

Game Theory in Everyday Life

Game Theory doesn't just work in games—it helps with real-life decisions too!

- **Taking turns:** If you always grab the best seat, your friends might stop letting you pick first. But if you take turns, everyone stays happy.
- **Negotiating:** If you and your sibling both want the last cookie, you can **offer to split it** instead of arguing and both getting in trouble.
- **Teamwork:** If you're playing soccer, **passing the ball at the right time** makes your team stronger instead of just trying to score alone.

Try It Yourself!

Imagine you and a friend are picking a movie to watch.

- **Without Game Theory:** You demand to watch what you want, but your friend refuses, and no one gets to watch anything.
- **With Game Theory:** You think ahead and say, *"Let's watch my choice today and your choice next time."* Now, both of you are happy!

Why Thinking Ahead Helps You Win

Game Theory **teaches you to predict what will happen next** so you can make the smartest choice. Whether you're playing a game, solving a problem, or working with others, **thinking ahead helps you succeed!**

Chapter 47: The Long View – Thinking About How Your Choices Affect the Future

Have you ever rushed through something just to get it over with, only to **wish you had taken more time**? Maybe you **scribbled down answers on a worksheet** just to finish quickly, but later you got them wrong. Or maybe you **picked the first idea for a project** instead of thinking it through, and later realized a different idea would have been much better.

That's why it's important to take **the long view**—which means **thinking beyond right now** and asking, *"How will this decision affect me later?"*

Why Quick and Easy Choices Aren't Always the Best

Some choices **feel like a good idea at the moment**, but later you might wish you had thought ahead.

- **Rushing through a test just to finish early** – You might make silly mistakes that you wouldn't have made if you had checked your work.
- **Picking the easiest book for a reading assignment** – You finish fast, but later you realize you didn't enjoy it or learn anything new.
- **Choosing not to practice for a big game** – You save time in the moment, but later you feel unprepared when it's time to play.

How to Think About the Future Before Deciding

Next time you have a choice to make, ask yourself:

1. **Will I still be happy with this decision tomorrow?** (*Example: If I rush through my project, will I be proud of my work later?*)
2. **Will this choice help me later on?** (*Example: If I practice a little each day, will I feel more confident when it really matters?*)
3. **If I take a little more time now, will it make things easier later?** (*Example: If I organize my backpack today, will I save time searching for things tomorrow?*)

Try It Yourself!

Imagine you're **building a puzzle.**

- **Short-term thinking:** You force the pieces together quickly, but they don't fit right, and you have to start over.
- **Long-term thinking:** You take your time and find the right pieces, so the puzzle comes together perfectly.

Why Thinking Ahead Helps You Succeed

When you take **the long view**, you make choices that **don't just feel good right now but also help you later.** Next time you're making a decision, **think beyond today—your future self will thank you!**

Chapter 48: Scenario Thinking – Imagining Different Futures Before You Decide

Have you ever watched someone **make a bad decision that could have been avoided** if they had just thought ahead? Maybe a friend signed up for too many activities and later felt overwhelmed, or someone started a big project without planning and ran out of time.

That's where **Scenario Thinking** helps! It's a way to **imagine different possibilities before making a choice** so you can avoid problems and prepare for success.

How Scenario Thinking Works

Before making a decision, ask yourself:
1. **What's the best thing that could happen?** (*Example: If I prepare for my speech, I'll feel confident and do well.*)

2. **What's the worst thing that could happen?** (*Example: If I don't practice, I might forget what to say and feel embarrassed.*)
3. **What's the most likely thing to happen?** (*Example: If I spend time practicing, I'll do fine, even if I feel a little nervous.*)

Why Scenario Thinking Helps You Make Smarter Choices

By imagining different possibilities, you can:

- **Avoid last-minute stress** by planning ahead.
- **Be better prepared** for challenges that might come up.
- **Make a choice that works for both now and later.**

Try It Yourself!

Imagine you're deciding **whether to join a new club at school.**

- **Best-case scenario:** You enjoy it, make new friends, and learn something cool.
- **Worst-case scenario:** It takes up too much time, and you struggle to keep up with your other work.
- **Most likely scenario:** If you manage your time wisely, you can participate and still balance your responsibilities.

A Smart Way to Plan for the Future

Scenario Thinking **helps you think ahead so you're ready for whatever happens.** The next time you're making a choice, **take a moment to picture different outcomes — so you can make the best decision possible!**

Chapter 49: Strategic Patience – Why Waiting Can Lead to Better Decisions

Have you ever been in a hurry to decide something, only to **wish you had waited a little longer**? Maybe you picked a book from the library quickly, but later found one you liked even more. Or maybe you answered a question in class too fast and realized **you knew a better answer** after thinking about it for a few more seconds.

That's where **Strategic Patience** helps! It means **waiting when it's the smart thing to do** — not because you're avoiding a decision, but because **a better choice might come if you give yourself time to think.**

Why Rushing Can Lead to Mistakes

Sometimes, making a quick decision **feels good in the moment** but doesn't work out in the long run.

- **Choosing the first idea that pops into your head** – You might come up with a better one if you take a little more time.
- **Answering a question too fast** – If you wait and think, you might remember something more accurate.
- **Saying "yes" to something without thinking** – You might realize later that you **don't actually have the time** or **don't really want to do it**.

How to Use Strategic Patience the Right Way

Strategic Patience **doesn't mean waiting forever** — it means knowing when to **pause and think before making a choice**.

1. **If a decision isn't urgent, give yourself time.** (*Example: If you're picking a book, take a few minutes to check different options before choosing.*)
2. **Ask yourself, "Do I really need to decide right now?"** (*Example: If someone asks for a favor, think about your schedule before saying yes immediately.*)
3. **Use waiting time wisely.** (*Example: If you're waiting to make a big decision, use the time to gather more information instead of just hoping for the best.*)

Try It Yourself!

Imagine you're deciding **which topic to choose for a school project.**

- **Without Strategic Patience:** You pick the first idea that comes to mind, but later realize it's not that interesting.
- **With Strategic Patience:** You take time to explore different topics and find one that's **really exciting and fun to work on.**

Why Waiting Can Lead to Smarter Choices

Strategic Patience **helps you avoid rushing into decisions you might regret.** The next time you have a choice to make, pause and give yourself time to think—you might come up with a much better idea!

Chapter 50: The Power of Experimentation – Testing Your Choices Before Committing

Have you ever wished you could **try something out before making a big decision**? What if you could test a sport before joining the team, or try out an instrument before committing to lessons? That's exactly what **experimentation** is all about!

Instead of guessing or making a choice you're unsure about, **experimentation lets you test things first** so you can make a smarter decision.

Why Experimenting Helps You Make Better Choices

Sometimes, it's hard to know if a choice is right until you've **actually tried it.**

- **Trying out a new hobby** – Instead of signing up for a whole season, you attend a trial class first.

- **Testing a new study method** – Before changing how you study, you try it for one test to see if it helps.
- **Exploring different interests** – Instead of assuming you won't like something, you give it a short try before deciding.

How to Use Experimentation in Decision-Making

Before making a big decision, ask yourself:

1. **Can I test this first before committing?** (*Example: If I'm unsure about joining a club, can I go to one meeting first?*)
2. **What small step can I take to see if this works?** (*Example: If I want to start running, can I try short runs before training for a race?*)
3. **How do I feel after trying it?** (*Example: Do I actually enjoy this, or do I want to try something else?*)

Try It Yourself!

Imagine you're deciding **whether to volunteer for a big event.**

- **Without Experimentation:** You sign up for a big role right away and later realize it's too much work.
- **With Experimentation:** You help out for a short time first, then decide whether you want to take on a bigger role.

Trust experience

Experimentation **helps you make decisions based on more than just guesses.** The next time you're unsure about something, **test it out first — then decide if it's right for you!**

Conclusion: What Makes a Great Decision-Maker? How to Keep Practicing Every Day!

By now, you've learned **so many ways** to make smart choices! You know how to **think ahead, stay calm, listen to others, and take responsibility** for your decisions. But the most important thing to remember is this: **Good decision-making is a skill— you get better at it the more you practice!**

What Great Decision-Makers Do

1. **They don't rush.** They **pause and think** before making a choice.
2. **They look at different options.** Instead of just picking the first idea, they **consider all the possibilities.**
3. **They ask for advice when needed.** They're not afraid to **listen and learn from others.**
4. **They aren't afraid of mistakes.** They know that **every choice is a chance to learn and improve.**

The more you **practice these skills in everyday life,** the easier it will be to make smart choices — big and small!

How to Keep Practicing

- **Play the "what if" game.** Ask yourself, *"What might happen if I make this choice?"*
- **Pause before deciding.** Give yourself a moment to think before jumping to a decision.

- **Learn from past choices.** If something didn't go well, think about what you could do differently next time.

Remember, **no one makes perfect choices all the time.** What matters most is that you keep **learning, thinking, and making the best choices you can!**

Appendices

1. Quick Reference Guide – A Cheat Sheet for Smart Decision-Making

Here's a **quick reminder** of the best tricks for making great choices!

Before You Decide, Ask Yourself:

What are my options? (*Is there more than one choice?*)

What could happen next? (*What are the good and bad results of each choice?*)

How will this choice affect me later? (*Will I still be happy with this decision tomorrow?*)

Am I feeling too emotional to decide? (*Should I take a break and think it over?*)

Do I need more information? (*Should I ask someone for advice?*)

If You're in a Group Decision:

Is everyone getting a chance to speak?

Are we thinking about all the options?

Are we choosing fairly, not just going with the loudest person's idea?

If You Make a Mistake:

What can I learn from this?

How can I make a better choice next time?

2. Practice Scenarios for Kids – Spot the Decision-Making Mistake Game!

Test your decision-making skills! Read each situation, find the mistake, and see how it can be fixed.

Scenario 1: The Rushed Choice

Liam is in a hurry to finish his homework, so he writes random answers without checking them. The next day, he realizes he made a lot of mistakes.

What went wrong?

Liam rushed through his work without taking time to check his answers, leading to mistakes.

Better choice:

Liam should slow down and take a few extra minutes to review his work. Even a quick check at the end can help catch mistakes and improve his answers.

Scenario 2: Ignoring Other Ideas

Samantha and her friends are picking a movie. Samantha insists on her choice and doesn't listen to anyone else. Some friends aren't happy.

What went wrong?

Samantha didn't consider what her friends wanted, which made the decision unfair.

Better choice:

Samantha should ask everyone for their opinions and look for a fair way to decide, like voting or taking turns choosing the movie.

Scenario 3: Not Thinking Ahead

Jordan spends all his free time playing outside and forgets to study for his test. When the test comes, he doesn't know the answers.

What went wrong?

Jordan didn't plan his time well and left his studying until it was too late.

Better choice:

Jordan should set aside a little time each day to review his notes. That way, he can still have fun outside while also being ready for the test.

Scenario 4: Letting Emotions Take Over

Mia is upset because her brother borrowed her markers without asking. She yells at him and takes one of his toys in return. Later, she feels bad.

What went wrong?

Mia reacted out of anger instead of solving the problem calmly.

Better choice:

Mia should take a deep breath and talk to her brother about how she feels. She can tell him why it upset her and ask him to ask permission next time.

Scenario 5: Making a Decision Without Enough Information

Ethan sees a cool-looking book at the library and checks it out without reading the summary or looking inside. When he gets home, he realizes he doesn't like it.

What went wrong?

Ethan picked a book without checking if it was something he would enjoy.

Better choice:

Ethan should take a moment to read the back cover or a few pages before choosing. This helps make sure the book is interesting to him.

Scenario 6: Avoiding Responsibility

Sophia is in a group project, but she forgets to do her part and doesn't tell her teammates. On the day of the presentation, the group is unprepared.

What went wrong?

Sophia didn't take responsibility for her task, which hurt the whole group.

Better choice:

Sophia should have let her team know she needed help or set a reminder to complete her part on time. When everyone in a group does their share, the project turns out better.

Scenario 7: Ignoring a Possible Problem

David and his friends are planning a picnic. The forecast says it might rain, but they don't make a backup plan. When it starts raining, they don't know what to do.

What went wrong?

David and his friends didn't prepare for the possibility of rain, which left them stuck.

Better choice:

They should have thought ahead and picked an indoor backup plan, like eating lunch in a covered area or at someone's house. Thinking about different outcomes helps avoid surprises.

3. Tips for Decision-Making –
The Top 10 Tricks for Choosing Wisely

1. **Take a deep breath before deciding.** (*A quick pause helps you think clearly!*)
2. **List your choices.** (*There's always more than one option!*)
3. **Think about what could happen next.** (*Good and bad results matter!*)
4. **Ask yourself: Will I still be happy with this choice later?**
5. **If it's a big decision, get advice from someone you trust.**
6. **If you're in a group, make sure everyone's voice is heard.**
7. **Use the "what if" test.** (*What if I wait? What if I choose differently?*)
8. **Don't let emotions take over.** (*If you're too angry, excited, or upset, wait before deciding!*)
9. **If you make a mistake, learn from it.** (*Mistakes are just lessons for next time!*)
10. **Practice, practice, practice!** (*The more you use these skills, the better you'll get!*)

Final Thought

Every day, you make **hundreds of decisions.** Some are small, like what to eat or wear. Others are big, like how to handle a challenge or solve a problem. No matter what the decision is, using these **smart decision-making skills** will help you **think clearly, make better choices, and feel more confident about the future!**

Here's another book by Quinn Voss that you might like